Under RIGOR in the Classroom

in the Classroom

Robert J. Marzano

1400 Centrepark Blvd, Suite 1000
West Palm Beach, FL 33401
717-845-6300

email: pub@learningsciences.com
learningsciences.com

Printed in the United States of America

21 20 19 18 17   1 2 3 4 5 6

Publisher's Cataloging-in-Publication Data
provided by Five Rainbows Cataloging Services

Names: Marzano, Robert J., author.
Title: Understanding rigor in the classroom / Robert Marzano.
Description: West Palm Beach, FL : Learning Sciences, 2019.
Identifiers: ISBN 978-1-943920-66-2 (paperback)
Subjects: LCSH: Teaching--Methodology. | Learning strategies. | Education--Aims and
objectives. | Effective teaching. | Education--Research. | BISAC: EDUCATION /
Teaching Methods & Materials / General. | EDUCATION / Professional Development.
Classification: LCC LB1025.3 .M339 2019 (print) | LCC LB1025.3 (ebook) | DDC
371.102--dc23.

Table of Contents

Chapter 3

Chapter 4

Chapter 5

Chapter 6

Chapter 7

The Nature of Rigor

The term *rigor* is ubiquitous in K–12 education, and one hears it bandied about as if it were a well-defined construct among educators. Unfortunately, this is not the case. Depending on which source you consult, you will encounter differing perspectives on what it means and how it is accomplished (see Blackburn, 2008; Hechinger Institute, 2009; Wagner 2008a, 2008b; Williamson & Johnston, 1999). In education, the term certainly became popular in the 1990s with the advent of the "rigor, relevance, and relationships" movement (see McNulty & Quaglia, 2007). I maintain that the precursor to the rigor, relevance, and relationships movement was the "thinking skills" movement of the 1980s that was initiated by the Association for Supervision and Curriculum Development (now known as ASCD) and cosponsored by the Association Collaborative for Teaching Thinking, which involved twenty-eight professional organizations including the American Educational Research Association, the National Council of Teachers of English, the International Reading Association (now the International Literacy Association), the National Council for Social Studies, the National Science Teachers Association, and the National Council of Teachers of Mathematics, among others. Although the term *rigor* was not a focal point of this initiative, many of the terms that are now used to define rigor were described and exemplified as a part of that effort. Those terms included *metacognitive skills*, *knowledge application skills*, *cognitive skills*, *habits of mind*, *dispositions*, and the like.

Regardless of the exact etymology of the term *rigor*, one thing is quite clear. If one is to propose techniques for enhancing rigor, one must define what is meant by rigor. In this book, I define it in a relatively straightforward manner. Rigor involves discerning new relationships between topics and new distinctions within topics. It also involves discerning new distinctions about oneself as a learner. I believe that everything currently discussed as being an aspect of rigor is secondary to these basic goals even though many of those things are noteworthy in their own right.

I should also note that the discussion in this book will exclude some strategies that have historically been thought of as standard fare when trying to enhance rigor. The most prominent of these exclusions is the use of "higher-order questions."

The Myth of Higher-Order Questions

One of the most enduring beliefs about enhancing rigor is that it can be developed simply by asking higher-order questions. Arguably, this perspective became prominent in the late 1970s and early 1980s when two related studies (Redfield & Rousseau, 1981; Winne, 1979) reported larger effect sizes for "higher-order" questions than for "lower-order" questions. Educators embraced this perspective quite readily and quickly, probably because it provided an easy solution to the problem of enhancing the complexity of students' thinking—simply ask higher-order questions.

In the years since, research has not supported the earlier beliefs about the benefits of higher-order questions and in fact refute the notion that higher-order questions produce more complex thinking (see Good & Brophy, 2003; Marzano & Simms, 2014; Wilen & Clegg, 1986). To illustrate, in 2014, Marzano and Simms conducted a synthesis of 39 studies that directly compared the effects of higher-order questions with lower-order questions: 21 of those studies found no difference, 10 of those studies found better effects for higher-order questions, and 8 of those studies found better effects for lower-order questions. In short, the simple use of questions as the primary approach to enhancing rigor is too simple in its application. Teachers must do far more than ask questions to improve the thinking of their students.

A Situated Perspective on Rigor

In this book I take the perspective that rigor is situational. Activities that spawn rigor in one situation are different from the activities that spawn rigor in a different situation. Furthermore, I take the perspective that the classroom situations in which rigor might occur can be defined by the interaction of two interacting variables: (1) the type of knowledge with which students are engaged and (2) how familiar students are with the content. We first consider the different types of knowledge.

Historically, cognitive scientists have made a distinction between declarative and procedural knowledge. Declarative knowledge is informational in nature. For example, the following statements that might be found in a state or local standards document are declarative in nature:

Mathematics: Understands the basic characteristics of a data distribution.

Literature: Can describe the defining characteristics of historical fiction.

Science: Understands the basic ways the sun supplies heat and light to the earth.

History: Can describe the circumstances that shaped the Civil War and its outcomes.

Procedural knowledge involves skills and processes. For example, the following statements that might be found in state and local standards documents are procedural in nature:

Mathematics: Is able to solve linear equations.

Writing: Edits a composition for overall logic.

Science: Is able to balance chemical equations.

Social Studies: Evaluates a persuasive article for its validity.

Being rigorous about declarative knowledge involves mental activities like discerning how one type of information is different from another type of information. For example, take the math concept of distributions. An activity that requires students to describe different types of distributions and what is similar and different about those types would deepen the level of rigor with which students understand the topic of distributions.

Being rigorous about procedural knowledge involves activities like breaking the steps into smaller parts. For example, consider the mental process of editing for overall logic. An activity that requires students to describe the process in terms of what you should do first, what you should do second, and so on would increase the rigor with which students execute the process.

The second dimension on which activities involving rigor can vary is how familiar students are with the content. When students are first introduced to an idea, activities involving rigor might be approached differently than how they would be if students have already acquired a basic understanding of the knowledge. Again, let's consider the declarative knowledge of distribution. If students are first being introduced to the topic of distributions in the context of a short video presentation, the teacher might cue them to continually ask themselves if they are confused about this new information and encourage them to turn these confusions into questions. This activity would increase the rigor of their initial understanding. We discuss this in Chapter 2. However, if students have previously been exposed to the concept of distribution, then the comparison activity just described, in which students describe similarities and differences for various distributions, would enhance the rigor of their understanding. We address this in Chapter 1.

Now let's reconsider the procedure knowledge of editing for overall logic. If students are newly learning this procedure, then helping them analyze the accuracy of the steps they employ would enhance rigor. We address this in Chapter 4. If students already have acquired a basic functionality with the procedure, then rigor is attained by helping them develop fluency as they execute the steps. We address this in Chapter 3.

In effect, then, there are four scenarios a teacher must consider when planning for instruction to enhance rigor. These are depicted in Table I.1:

Table I.1. *Four classroom situations to enhance rigor*

	Initial Learning of Content	After Initial Learning of Content
Declarative Knowledge	Plan activities that enhance rigor while students are initially learning declarative knowledge.	Plan activities that enhance rigor after students have initially learned declarative knowledge.
Procedural Knowledge	Plan activities that enhance rigor while students are initially learning procedural knowledge.	Plan activities that enhance rigor after students have initially learned procedural knowledge.

Table I.1 depicts the four situations that will be the focus of this book. The first four chapters articulate specific rigor-enhancing strategies for each of these four scenarios.

Using Cognitive Analysis Processes and Habits of Mind

In this book, I use two types of activities that can be employed within the four previously described scenarios: cognitive analysis processes and habits of mind.

Cognitive Analysis Processes

When used properly, cognitive analysis processes help students analyze knowledge in depth. These processes have been used for decades as tools for fostering higher-level thinking (see Marzano et al., 1988). For the purposes of this book, we focus on the five cognitive analysis processes listed in Table I.2:

Table I.2. *Cognitive analysis skills*

Cognitive Analysis Skill	Description
Comparing	Identifying how two items are similar and/or different relative to specific characteristics
Classifying	Identifying the category an item belongs to based on specific characteristics or grouping items into categories based on specific characteristics
Supporting Claims	Building a hierarchic system of support for statements believed to be true
Elaborating	Inferring characteristics based on assumptions or inferring consequences based on reasoning
Analyzing Errors	Identifying common errors in reasoning or errors in the execution of a procedure

As will be described in Chapters 1 through 4, these cognitive analysis processes can be applied to both declarative and procedural knowledge when they are initially being learned and after they have been initially learned. As we will see in Chapter 5, they can also be considered an explicit part of the curriculum and taught directly.

Habits of Mind

The habits have also been used for decades as tools not only for deepening students' understanding of content, but also for increasing their metacognitive awareness (Marzano et al., 1988). They are commonly referred to as *habits of mind* and as *dispositions*. In this book, I use both labels but will more commonly refer to them as habits of mind. Table I.3 lists the habits of mind featured in this book.

The dispositions can be used in tandem with the cognitive analysis processes to enhance rigor with declarative and procedural knowledge when they are initially learned and after they are learned. Chapters 1 through 4 describe

Table I.3. *Habits of mind*

Habits of Mind	Description
Staying focused when answers and solutions are not apparent	Recognizing you have become frustrated because you can't find an answer or solution and continuing to try
Seeking accuracy	Recognizing when it's important to be accurate and seeking sources to confirm your accuracy
Resisting impulsivity	Recognizing when you are making decisions or generating conclusions too quickly
Seeking clarity	Recognizing when you do not understand important content and taking steps to clear up misunderstandings
Developing fluency	Recognizing when you must balance speed and accuracy when executing a procedure and taking steps to do so
Seeking cohesion and coherence	Recognizing when content is composed of small units that interact to form a unified whole and attending to both
Taking incremental steps	Recognizing when a situation involves multiple steps that cannot be approached as a whole and breaking it into smaller parts

their use. They can also be taught directly as part of the curriculum. This is described in Chapter 6.

Identifying the Classroom Situation

A hard but overlooked fact about fostering rigor is that it requires thoughtful planning on the part of teachers. A basic premise of this book is that planning for rigor must involve identifying the specific classroom situation within which rigor will be addressed. Once this is done, specific cognitive analysis processes and specific habits of mind can be selected to create rigor-producing activities for students.

The planning process and its resulting decisions described in this book are summarized in Table I.4.

Table I.4. *Rigor planning process*

What type of content will I be addressing: declarative or procedural?	
Declarative	**Procedural**
If students are initially learning the declarative content, use the following cognitive analysis processes:	If students are initially learning the procedural content, use the following cognitive analysis processes:
• Analyzing errors • Elaborating	• Analyzing errors • Elaborating
Use the following habits of mind:	Use the following habits of mind:
• Seeking clarity • Seeking accuracy	• Seeking clarity • Taking incremental steps
If students have already been introduced to the declarative content, use the following cognitive analysis processes:	If students have already been introduced to the procedural content, use the following cognitive analysis processes:
• Comparing • Classifying • Constructing support	• Comparing • Classifying
Use the following habits of mind:	Use the following habits of mind:
• Staying focused when answers and solutions aren't apparent • Resisting impulsivity	• Developing fluency • Seeking cohesion and coherence

What You Will Find in This Book

Chapters 1 through 4 address the four classroom scenarios in which rigor might be addressed. Chapter 5 introduces the topic of teaching the cognitive analysis processes as content in their own right, and Chapter 6 addresses teaching the habits of mind as content in their own right. Finally, Chapter 7 addresses how project-based instruction can be used as a vehicle for enhancing rigor. In effect, this book attempts to provide a focused, yet comprehensive, framework for enhancing rigor across grade levels and subject areas.

CHAPTER 1

Rigor with Declarative Knowledge

After students have initially learned a topic, the most common situation in which classroom teachers try to enhance rigor is with declarative knowledge. There are at least two reasons for this. First, declarative knowledge is the most common form of content articulated in standards documents. Although this might not seem obvious, previous research makes it quite clear. To illustrate, consider Table 1.1.

Table 1.1. *Amount of declarative versus procedural standards across subject areas*

Subject	Declarative		Procedural	
Mathematics	139		84	
English Language Arts (ELA)	86		254	
Science	253		8	
History	1,240		41	
Geography	230		8	
Arts	147		122	
Civics	426		1	
Economics	159		0	
Foreign Language	52		56	
Health	121		15	
Physical Education	47		58	
Behavioral Studies	100		0	
Technology	106		38	
Life Skills	67		241	
Total	3,173	77.41%	926	22.59%

Note: Results computed from data in McREL International, 2014a, 2014b.

As depicted in Table 1.1, most subject areas have a majority of content that is declarative, with the exceptions of English Language Arts (ELA), the arts, foreign language, physical education, and life skills. What is surprising is the sheer amount of declarative knowledge. Across the fourteen subject areas reported in Table 1.1, 77.41% of the content is declarative in nature.

A second reason is that teachers quite naturally think of working on rigor with specific content after students have initially learned it. This is because we typically think of rigor as going into more depth. For example, consider the concept of percolation in science. We tend to think that students have to learn an easy version of percolation before they can do something with it that is more complex.

As stated in the introductory chapter, my perspective is that rigor can be enhanced after students have initially learned something and while they are first learning something. We address rigor when initially learning declarative knowledge in Chapter 2. Here we consider rigor after students have been introduced to declarative knowledge.

Identify the Specific Topics on Which You Will Focus

Over the years I've come to the conclusion that rigor, regarding declarative knowledge, is achieved only after teachers have identified specific topics on which they will focus. In a single unit and even in a single lesson, a wide variety of explicit and implicit topics might be presented to students. Rigor cannot be achieved with all of these topics or even a few topics simultaneously. Consequently, teachers must identify a specific topic or two on which to focus as their first order of business. Table 1.2 lists some of the common types of topics teachers identify relative to declarative knowledge.

Prior to planning instruction to enhance rigor, a teacher should identify the specific declarative types of topics on which he or she will focus. With this level of focus established, the teacher can employ various cognitive analysis processes to enhance rigor.

Using the Cognitive Analysis Processes

As described in the introductory chapter, cognitive analysis processes have a long history in K–12 education. In this book, we employ five of those processes: comparing, classifying, constructing support, analyzing errors, and elaborating. All of these can be used with virtually all types of knowledge. However, some fit more readily with certain types of knowledge in certain situations. In this chapter, we address comparing, classifying, and constructing support as they relate to enhancing rigor with declarative knowledge after students have initially learned it.

Table 1.2. *Types of topics for declarative knowledge*

Topic	Examples
Specific persons or type of person	Abraham Lincoln, US President
Specific organization or type of organizations	New York Yankees, professional baseball team
Specific intellectual or artistic product or type of intellectual or artistic product	*Mona Lisa*, famous painting
Specific naturally occurring object or type of naturally occurring object	Linden tree, tree
Specific naturally occurring place or type of naturally occurring place	Arctic Ocean, ocean
Specific animal or type of animal	Secretariat, famous race horse
Specific manmade object or type of manmade object	Rolls-Royce, expensive passenger automobile
Specific manmade place or type of manmade place	Roman Colosseum, sports arena
Specific naturally occurring phenomenon or event or type of naturally occurring phenomenon or event	Mount St. Helens eruption, volcanic eruption
Specific manmade phenomenon or event or type of manmade phenomenon or event	Macy's Thanksgiving Day Parade, holiday event
Specific manmade abstraction or type of abstraction	Linear function, function; love, emotion

Comparing

With one or two target topics identified, it is fairly easy to engage students in comparing activities designed to enhance rigor. Technically, *comparison* means that you're examining how items are similar, whereas *contrast* means that you are examining how items are different. Here I use the common convention of referring to the identification of both similarities and/or differences as comparing.

Comparing tasks should be set up in a thoughtful manner and become more complex and rigorous as you move up through the grades. At the primary level, the teacher might design comparison tasks using the following process:

▶ The teacher identifies the topics to be compared.

▶ The teacher identifies simple characteristics on which to compare the topics.

- The teacher asks students to describe how the topics are similar and/or different.
- The teacher asks students to summarize what they have learned and describe how their thinking has changed.

To illustrate, the following is a primary-level comparing task for the topics of mammals and birds a teacher might design.

> After studying mammals and some of their characteristics, the teacher asks students to respond to the following question to compare what they had just studied about mammals in this unit with what they studied about birds in the previous unit:
>
> How are mammals and birds similar and different in terms of:
>
> - How their offspring are born?
> - Their body coverings?
> - Their extremities?

Students could be asked to answer these questions from memory, but the activity is more powerful in terms of enhancing rigor if students are allowed to use resources to answer the comparing prompt. For example, the teacher might guide students to preselected and screened websites. Students would find and report answers like the following:

- Mammals give live birth, but birds lay eggs.
- Mammal have fur or hair, but birds have feathers.
- Mammals feed their young milk produced by their bodies, but birds feed their young by regurgitating partially digested food.

Relative to the last part of the activity in which students are asked to summarize what they have learned and explain how their thinking has changed, one student might note that she knew about the difference between mammals and birds in terms of their extremities and how their offspring were born but had never really thought about how mammals and birds feed their young.

At the upper elementary and middle school levels, the teacher designs comparison tasks that involve more abstract characteristics. The task design process at this level includes the following:

- The teacher identifies the items to be compared.
- The teacher identifies complex or abstract characteristics on which to compare the items.

- The teacher asks students to describe how the topics are similar and/or different.
- The teacher asks students to summarize what they have learned and describe how their thinking has changed.

To change the primary comparison task about mammals and birds to a task appropriate for the upper elementary and middle school levels, the teacher would add characteristics that are more complex and abstract, like the following:

- The difference in how they produce sound (Answer: Mammals produce sound through their larynx; birds have a syrinx, which serves as a voice box.)
- The difference in their bone structure (Answer: Mammals have solid, more dense bones; birds have hollow bones.)

At the high school level, the teacher identifies the items to be compared but then has students identify the characteristics by which to compare them and justify why those characteristics are important to understanding the items. The task design process at the high school level includes the following:

- The teacher identifies the items to be compared.
- The teacher asks students to identify complex or abstract characteristics on which to compare the items and justify why those characteristics are important to understanding the items.
- The teacher asks students to describe how the items are similar and/or different.
- The teacher asks students to summarize what they have learned and describe how their thinking has changed.

To illustrate, consider the following task.

A high school teacher provides students with the topics of mammals and birds, which they have addressed in a unit on diversity of life. The teacher charges students with identifying the characteristics on which to compare them, but emphasizes the fact that the characteristics they select should provide new insights into the two types of animals not addressed in the unit. Student reporting focuses on explaining how the characteristics they have selected provide these new insights.

As these examples illustrate, across the grade levels, characteristics become more abstract and complex and students are assigned more responsibility in the design of the comparing tasks. Other ways to manipulate the difficulty of comparing tasks include

- using increasingly more abstract or complete topics; and
- using three or more topics in the comparison task.

Classifying

As noted in the introductory chapter, classifying can be addressed from two different perspectives. One involves identifying the categories within a topic. This is referred to as subordinate classifying. The other perspective is identifying the category to which a topic belongs. This is referred to as superordinate classifying.

Subordinate Classifying

Subordinate classifying involves identifying categories within a target topic. For example, consider the topic of common nouns. Possible subordinate categories within this topic include:

- Abstract nouns ("bravery")
- Collective nouns ("team")
- Compound nouns ("water bottle")
- Concrete nouns ("tree")
- Uncountable noun ("music")
- Gender-specific nouns ("actress")
- Countable nouns ("an attack")
- Gerunds ("running")

Sometimes, subordinate categories (i.e., subcategories) are well defined and sometimes they are not. At the primary level, the task design process for subordinate classifying includes the following:

- The teacher identifies the topic on which to focus.
- The teacher identifies the subcategories within the topic.
- The teacher presents students with items that fit into various subcategories.
- Students are asked to sort the items into the identified subcategories.
- The teacher asks students to summarize what they have learned and describe how their thinking has changed.

To illustrate this process, consider the following task.

A teacher has introduced the topic of common nouns to students. The teacher designs a task that presents students with the following examples of common nouns and asks them to classify them as a concrete noun, a collective noun, or a compound noun:

- Paper clip
- Mother-in-law
- Animal
- Team
- Bench
- Post office
- Choir
- Car
- Crowd

At the upper elementary and middle school levels, the teacher identifies the topic and then asks students to identify at least some of the subcategories within the topic. The task design process at this level includes the following:

- The teacher identifies the topic on which to focus.
- The teacher provides students with some of the subcategories and asks students to identify at least one other subcategory.
- The teacher asks students to identify items that fit into the subcategories and defend their choices.
- The teacher asks students to summarize what they have learned and describe how their thinking has changed.

To illustrate, consider the following task.

The teacher presents students with the following categories of nouns: common nouns, proper nouns, and count nouns. The teacher also asks students to identify at least one other category of nouns. The teacher then asks students to identify examples of common nouns, proper nouns, count nouns, and the category students provided and defend why the examples they have selected fit into a specific category.

At the high school level, the teacher identifies the topic and asks students to identify traditional and nontraditional categories within the topic. The task design process at this level includes the following:

- The teacher identifies the topic on which to focus.
- The teacher asks students to identify the subcategories within the topic with the provision that some categories need to be those that are not commonly associated with the topic.

> ▸ The teacher asks students to identify items that fit into the subcategories and defend their choices.

> ▸ The teacher asks students to summarize what they have learned and describe how their thinking has changed.

To illustrate, consider the following task.

An English teacher supplies students with the initial topic of nouns, but then asks them to define at least five traditional categories of nouns they are aware of and examples of the elements within. In addition, students are asked to create at least one new category that is not considered to be a traditional category and provide examples of items that fall within this category. Students are asked to explain what the new category adds to the understanding of nouns. For example, a student might identify the nontraditional category of emotional nouns such as hate or love. The student might defend this category as shedding light on the fact that noun categories help organize types of human experiences.

As is the case with all cognitive analysis processes, the task design process for subordinate classifying gradually releases responsibility to students for identifying categories and the items that fit within those categories. In addition, students at the high school level are asked to generate new categories into which a topic might fall and analyze how the perspective adds insight into the topic.

Other ways to manipulate the complexity of subordinate classifying tasks include

> ▸ using more abstract or complex topics; and

> ▸ requiring students to go to multiple levels of categories and subcategories

Superordinate Classifying

As its name implies, superordinate classifying involves identifying categories into which target topics belong. At the primary level, the task design process includes the following:

> ▸ The teacher identifies the superordinate category into which the topic belongs.

> ▸ The teacher identifies the characteristics of that superordinate category.

> ▶ The teacher asks students to describe how the characteristics of the superordinate category apply to the topic.
> ▶ The teacher asks students to summarize what they have learned and describe how their thinking has changed.

To illustrate, consider the following task.

The teacher reads Aesop's *The Owl and the Grasshopper* to the students. The teacher explains that this is a type of fable and that a fable has the following characteristics:

- a good lesson for us to learn from;
- benefits of learning the lesson;
- a wise character who learns the lesson;
- a lazy or foolish character who does not learn the lesson; and
- an outdoor, countryside setting.

Students are asked to provide examples of these characteristics in *The Owl and Grasshopper*.

At the upper elementary and middle school levels, the teacher identifies a superordinate category into which the target topic falls and then asks students to identify and apply the characteristic of that category. The task design process at this level includes the following:

> ▶ The teacher identifies the topic and the superordinate category to which it belongs.
> ▶ The teacher asks students to describe the characteristics of that superordinate category.
> ▶ The teacher asks students to describe how the characteristics of the superordinate category manifest in the topic.
> ▶ The teacher asks students to summarize what they have learned and describe how their thinking has changed.

To illustrate, consider the following task.

After students have read *Lunch-Box Dream* by Tony Abbott, the teacher informs them that this is a historical novel. Students are asked to look up the characteristics of historical novels and then describe how they are exemplified in *Lunch-Box Dream*.

At the high school level, the teacher asks students to examine a topic from the perspective of two or more categories into which the topic might fall, along with the defining characteristics of the categories. The task design process at this level includes the following:

- The teacher identifies two or more categories into which the target topic might be classified.
- The teacher asks students to describe the defining characteristics of each of the categories.
- The teacher asks students to describe how each classification provides a unique perspective on the topic.
- The teacher asks students to summarize what they have learned and describe how their thinking has changed.

To illustrate, consider the following task.

Students have read the novel *The Chocolate War* by Robert Cormier. The teacher presents them with the following categories: psychological thriller, realism, Gothic literature, and tragedy. Students are asked to select two of these and describe the defining characteristics of each. They then describe how *The Chocolate War* exhibits the defining characteristics of each specific category. They also describe how each category provides a unique perspective on the novel.

The driving force underlying all superordinate classifying tasks is that the characteristics of the superordinate category shed light on the target topic. There are a variety of ways other than task design to manipulate the complexity of superordinate classifying tasks, including

- having students design unique superordinate categories; and
- using multiple superordinate categories.

Constructing Support

The cognitive analysis process of constructing support falls into the broader category of argumentation which, of course, can be viewed from the perspective of a form of writing and as a tool for persuasion. Here we focus on the more specific process of providing support for a claim and how it can be used to enhance rigor.

A claim is made every time we assert that we believe something to be true. Of course, this happens frequently in the course of a single day or even a single class period. To execute the cognitive analysis process of constructing support, students must understand its nature. More specifically, well-designed support for a claim involves three components:

Grounds: Initial reasons that support a claim. They answer the question, *Why do you think your claim is true?*

Backing: Additional information about the grounds that support their validity. Backing is more detailed and more specific than grounds and can involve in-depth evidence such as research-based data, expert opinion, and statistical analyses.

Qualifier: Exceptions to the claim. These exceptions describe situations in which the claim is probably not true.

At the primary level, students would not be required to demonstrate all the components of support, but they might be expected to provide simplified grounds. The task design process at the primary level includes the following:

▶ The teacher provides students with a claim about the target topic.

▶ The teacher asks students to provide a few reasons or grounds supporting or not supporting the claim.

▶ The teacher asks students to summarize what they have learned and describe how their thinking has changed.

To illustrate, consider the following task.

Students have been learning about the topic of eating balanced meals. The teacher provides the following claim: *The lunches in our school are balanced meals.* Students are asked to provide reasons (grounds) why they believe this claim is true or reasons (grounds) why they believe it is not true.

At the upper elementary and middle school levels, students are asked to address both grounds and backing. The task design process at this level includes the following:

▶ The teacher provides students with a claim regarding a specific topic.

▶ The teacher asks students to provide reasons (grounds) supporting or not supporting the claim.

▶ The teacher asks students to provide evidence (backing) that provide evidence for their reasons (grounds).

▶ The teacher asks students to summarize what they have learned and describe how their thinking has changed.

To illustrate, consider the following task.

> The teacher presents students with the following claim in science class: *Many scientific innovations have had a hard time being accepted because of the common beliefs during the time in which they were developed.* Students are asked to provide one or more reasons (grounds) that support or do not support this claim as well as one or more pieces of evidence (backing) supporting each reason.

At the high school level, the teacher expects students to utilize the entire process of constructing support. The task design process at this level includes the following:

- The teacher presents students with a topic.
- The teacher asks students to generate a claim regarding the topic.
- The teacher asks students to come up with two or more grounds.
- The teacher asks students to provide backing for each of the grounds.
- The teacher asks students to design qualifiers as needed.
- The teacher asks students to summarize what they have learned and describe how their thinking has changed.

To illustrate, consider the following task.

> The teacher asks students to pick a common health care product advertised on television. Students articulate a claim about that product along with grounds and backing for the claim. Students are also asked to consider if each of their grounds requires some type of qualifier and to provide one if necessary.

Task design for constructing support requires students to use more and more of the full process as they progress through the grade levels. Other than task design process, there are a number of ways to manipulate the complexity of constructing support tasks, including

- having students collect grounds and backing from a variety of sources; and
- providing more complex claims.

Summarizing What You Have Learned and Describing How Your Thinking Has Changed

It is important to note that every cognitive analysis process described in this book ends with students summarizing what they have learned and describing how their thinking has changed. This activity helps solidify students' thinking and ensures that they ascertain some new distinctions about the content. Such distinctions are the essence of rigor.

A teacher can facilitate this part of the cognitive analysis processes by asking students to respond to the following questions:

- What was I right about regarding this topic?
- What was I wrong about regarding this topic?
- What additions do I need to make to my understanding of this topic?

Using the Habits of Mind

While it is true that just about any habit of mind can be used with just about any type of task, here we consider two specific dispositions that fit well with the cognitive analysis processes described in this chapter. They are staying focused when answers and solutions are not immediately apparent and resisting impulsivity.

Staying Focused When Answers and Solutions Are Not Apparent

Staying focused when answers and solving are not apparent can be thought of as a specific instantiation of persistence. Like all the other habits of mind, this can be taught and reinforced as students are engaged in cognitive analysis processes.

When a teacher wants students to practice a specific disposition in the context of a specific cognitive analysis task, he or she should first provide students with a set of steps that walk students through the habit of mind and then gradually make those steps more sophisticated. We consider how to do this in Chapter 6. The following is a step-by-step process the teacher might initially use to help students stay focused when answers and solutions are not apparent:

- Ask yourself: *What am I trying to accomplish right now?*
- Try to describe what is frustrating you or what it is you can't find or solve.
- Tell yourself you are going to give it at least one more try and then do so.
- When you're done, summarize what you have learned about yourself.

Initially, the teacher should talk students through the steps of this process. For example, while students are engaged in a particularly difficult comparison task, the teacher might interrupt them and ask them to determine if they are getting frustrated. The teacher would continue by explaining that if they are getting frustrated, they should remind themselves of their goal and try to determine what is stopping them in this particular task. In a comparison task, students might find it hard to describe how topics are similar and/or different relative to a specific characteristic. This might mean they need to seek some information about the characteristics. The teacher would continually reinforce the central tenet of staying focused when answers and solutions are not apparent, which is to keep attending to the issue and keep trying.

Over time, the teacher would ask students to use this process more and more independently with the goal that it becomes habitual. Occasionally, the teacher might also ask students to fill out a simple self-evaluation scale like the following:

4. I've been staying focused on my own when answers and solutions are not immediately apparent to me without any teacher reminders.

3. I've been aware of when I'm losing my focus when answers and solutions aren't immediately apparent to me, but I still don't do a good job of refocusing my attention.

2. I've been trying to stay focused when the teacher reminds me, but not otherwise.

1. I really haven't been trying to stay focused at all when I can't find an answer or solution.

Resisting Impulsivity

The habit of mind of resisting impulsivity helps us avoid making decisions or forming conclusions without proper consideration. The teacher can initially provide the following step-by-step process to students:

▶ Stop for a moment and think about what you're about to do.

▶ Ask yourself, *Is there anything about what I'm thinking of doing that I should reconsider?*

▶ Once you've thought about your reaction, go ahead and act.

▶ When you're done, summarize what you have learned about yourself.

The teacher might walk students through this process while they are involved in a constructing support task. The teacher might explain that it's easy to fall into the trap of simply listing grounds for a claim and quickly coming up with backing. The teacher might explain that the second step of the process is particularly powerful because it reminds us to carefully consider whether the grounds or backing we are considering really provide proper support. Occasionally, the teacher might ask student to rate themselves using the following scale:

4. I've been resisting impulsivity without any teacher reminders.

3. I've been aware of when I'm acting impulsively, but I still don't do a good job of stopping to think more deeply.

2. I've been trying to resist impulsivity when the teacher reminds me, but not otherwise.

1. I really haven't been trying to resist impulsivity.

Revisiting Higher-Order Questions

In the introductory chapter, I made the point that the concept of higher-order questions is basically flawed. Although the idea of asking higher-order questions has some intuitive appeal, the manner in which it has been historically executed doesn't work because it overly simplifies what it takes to stimulate deeper thinking on the part of students. However, if one takes into consideration the type of knowledge that is the focus of instruction (i.e., declarative or procedural) and the cognitive processes or habits of mind that are being employed, questions can be constructed that more directly and pointedly stimulate higher-order thinking which, as we have seen, is closely aligned with what I refer to as rigor in this book.

Rather than use the term higher-order questions, I prefer to use the terms *cognitive analysis questions* and *habits of mind questions* simply because these terms specify the process that is the target of the questions. Cognitive analysis questions relate to questions that stimulate the various cognitive analysis processes. Habits of mind questions focus on the habits of mind. Another legitimate name for these questions could be metacognitive questions because they focus students' attention on their attitudes and beliefs as well as their thinking processes. In Chapter 6 we address the metacognitive nature of the habits of mind in some depth.

Cognitive Analysis Questions

As described previously, each cognitive analysis task ends with students being asked to summarize what they have learned and describe how their thinking has changed. The questions described in this section provide a focus for this activity that is directly related to the type of cognitive analysis task.

Questions that might be used with comparing tasks include:

- What are some similarities in these topics that you were previously not aware of?
- What are some differences in these topics that you were previously not aware of?
- Which were harder to identify: similarities or differences? Why?

Questions that might be used with subordinate classifying tasks include:

- What are some subcategories within this topic you were not aware of?
- What are some characteristics of the topic you were not aware of?
- What was most difficult about identifying subcategories for this topic? Why?

Questions that might be used for superordinate classifying tasks include:

- What were some of the superordinate categories for this topic you were not aware of?
- What are some characteristics of this topic you were not aware of?
- What was most difficult about identifying superordinate categories for this topic? Why?

Questions that might be used with constructing support tasks include:

- What are some aspects of this claim you were not aware of?
- What are some aspects of the grounds or backing you were not aware of?
- What are some aspects of the qualifier you were not aware of?
- What was the most difficult part of supporting this claim? Why?

Habits of Mind Questions

Habits of mind questions require students to take a deep look at themselves as learners and, to this extent, are metacognitive by definition. Students should be taught the habits and receive practice in their use. We discuss this in Chapter 6. Once they begin to understand and use the habits of mind, teachers can cue their use by asking questions.

Questions that might be used with the habit of mind of staying focused when answers and solutions are not apparent include:

- What things do you become aware of that let you know you should try to stay focused even though answers and solutions are not apparent?

- When you realize that you can't find answers or solutions, what emotions do you feel and what do you say to yourself?
- What is one small action you could take to get better at staying focused when answers and solutions aren't apparent?

It is important to note that all habits of mind questions involve an awareness of our emotions and what we say to ourselves in situations where a particular habit of mind should be used. Again, we consider this issue in depth in Chapter 6 where we address the importance of "inner dialogue" as a form metacognitive self-control.

Questions that might be used with the habit of mind of resisting impulsivity include:

- What things do you become aware of that let you know you should resist impulsivity?
- When you realize you are being impulsive, what emotions do you feel and what do you say to yourself?
- What is one small thing you could do to get better at resisting impulsivity?

Summary

This chapter addressed enhancing rigor with declarative knowledge once students have initially been introduced to such knowledge. A critical step in the process is for the teacher to identify a few topics to be the focus of rigor. With target topics identified, a teacher designs rigor-enhancing tasks using the cognitive analysis process of comparing, subordinate classifying, superordinate classifying, and constructing support. These tasks become more abstract and complex as they progress up through the grade levels. They also become more student directed. Specific habits of mind can also be taught and reinforced in the context of cognitive analysis tasks. The chapter addressed how the disposition of staying focused when answers and solutions are not apparent and the disposition of resisting impulsivity should be employed in such tasks. Finally, this chapter presented questions that can used to deepen students' learning relative to the cognitive analysis processes and the habits of mind.

CHAPTER 2

Rigor When Initially Learning Declarative Knowledge

In Chapter 1, we addressed enhancing rigor with declarative knowledge after students have been introduced to it. In this chapter, we address enhancing rigor when students are initially learning declarative knowledge. Of course, the distinction between initially learning declarative knowledge versus then developing deeper levels of understanding afterward is somewhat of an artificial one. Clearly, there is no exact point at which we have initially learned content. This noted, it is useful to make the distinction for instructional planning purposes.

It is important to remember that Chapter 1 began with the mandate that teachers identify a topic or two on which to focus. The discussion in this chapter is based on the assumption that a teacher has done just that. If students have already been introduced to the identified topics, then the teacher would use the cognitive analysis process described in Chapter 1. However, if students have not been introduced to the identified topics, then the teacher would use the cognitive analysis processes described here.

Initially learning declarative knowledge involves obtaining a sense of the characteristics of the declarative topic. More technically, as we learn about a new declarative topic, we create an internal representation of the information. This representation can be loosely referred to as a *mental model* and more technically referred to as a *macrostructure* (see Kintsch, 1974, 1979; Kintsch & van Dijk, 1978; Marzano, 1992; Marzano et al., 1988). For the purposes of this book, teachers should remain aware that, when students are initially learning about a new topic, they should start by understanding a few critical characteristics and gradually expand on and refine what they know. In effect, it is probably accurate to say that we never stop learning about a declarative topic as long as we continue to receive information about the topic.

Using the Cognitive Analysis Processes

There are two cognitive analysis processes that fit well when students are initially learning declarative knowledge in that they help students expand on their initial understanding of a topic: elaborating and analyzing errors.

Elaborating (Default Elaborations)

There are two types of elaborations that can be applied to knowledge. One type of elaboration involves inferring characteristics based on assumptions, termed *default elaboration*. The other type involves inferring consequences based on reasoning and is referred to as *reasoned elaborations*. We should note that the process of elaboration is a type of inference. Therefore, I will use the terms *default elaborations* and *default inferences* synonymously, and the terms *reasoned elaborations* and *reasoned inferences* synonymously.

Default elaborations occur when a student automatically assumes that certain characteristics are associated with a particular topic. For example, when students watch a video about a particular type of insect, they might immediately assume that the insect has the following characteristics:

- They have a shell-like covering on the outside of the body.
- They have antennae on the top of their heads.
- They crawl or fly.

They make these default inferences because they know characteristics about insects and assume that those characteristics apply to any new type of insect they are learning about. We do the same thing when we encounter information about people. For example, we meet someone who is a firefighter and we assume she is in good physical shape, faces dangerous situations, and is brave. This is because we associate the following characteristics with firefighters:

- They keep themselves in good physical condition.
- They routinely put themselves in dangerous situations.
- They are brave.

These examples involve knowing something about the category to which a topic belongs. Default elaborations also occur when we've already learned a little bit about topic and subconsciously fill in details. For example, if we've been introduced to the topic of snow leopards and know a little bit about them, we may automatically start assuming characteristics about them that make intuitive sense to us. From these perspectives, then, default elaborations are one of the first ways we learn about new topics. We automatically "fill in the blanks" based on our assumptions and store this information in our long-term memories.

A teacher can help students access this stored information as they learn new declarative knowledge through direct questions that are designed to identify what students think they know. These assumptions can then be analyzed for their accuracy. This is done through focused and well-structured questions. To aid in the creation of such questions, I recommend that teachers use the question prompts in Table 2.1.

Table 2.1 lists common topics for which a teacher might design default elaboration questions. For each topic, a set of prompts is provided. For example, assume the teacher is introducing the topic of the eruption of Mount St. Helens in 1980. The teacher knows that students have heard of that eruption but doesn't know the extent of their prior knowledge or how accurate that knowledge is. The teacher consults Table 2.1, decides that the eruption of Mount St. Helens can be considered a type of naturally occurring phenomenon, and finds a set of generic questions on this type of topic:

  ▸ What places are associated with this phenomenon?
  ▸ What time period is associated with this phenomenon?
  ▸ What causes or consequences are associated with this phenomenon?
  ▸ What happened during this phenomenon?

The teacher then translates these general questions into more specific questions:

  ▸ Which specific towns and cities were most affected by the Mt. St. Helens eruption?
  ▸ When were the first major signs that Mt. St. Helens would erupt, and what were the signs?
  ▸ What was the immediate impact of the eruption in Washington State and across the country?
  ▸ What happened during the first 24 hours of the eruption?

Using these questions, the teacher can determine what students believe they know about the topic and then use that information to help deepen their understanding of the topic. In effect, the question stems in Table 2.1 help teachers construct default elaboration tasks that enhance rigor.

At the primary level, the design process for default elaboration tasks includes the following:

  ▸ The teacher identifies how students will receive new information about the target topic (e.g., listen to a presentation, read about it, watch a video, look up information on the Internet).
  ▸ The teacher structures specific questions for students to answer that will cue them to make default inferences.

Table 2.1. *Common types of default questions*

Topic	Default Questions
Specific person or type of person (Abraham Lincoln, US president)	What *time period* is associated with this person? What *places* are associated with this person? What *events* are associated with this person? What *accomplishments* are associated with this person?
Specific organization or type of organization (New York Yankees, professional baseball team)	What *beliefs* are associated with this organization or group? What *locations* are associated with this organization or group? What *time period* is associated with this organization or group? What *events* are associated with this organization or group?
Specific intellectual or artistic product or type of intellectual or artistic product (*Mona Lisa*, famous painting)	What *person* is associated with this product? What *time period* is associated with this product? What *event* is associated with this product? What *causes or consequences* are associated with this product? What *places* are associated with this product? What *values* are associated with this product?
Specific naturally occurring object or type of naturally occurring object (Linden tree, tree)	What *events* are associated with this object? What *people* are associated with this object? What *time period* is associated with this object? What *location* is associated with this object?
Specific naturally occurring place or type of naturally occurring place (Arctic Ocean, ocean)	What *events* are associated with this place? What *people* are associated with this place? What *time period* is associated with this place? What *location* is associated with this place?
Specific animal or type of animal (Secretariat, famous race horse)	What *events* are associated with this animal? What *people* are associated with this animal? What *time period* is associated with this animal? What *locations* are associated with this animal? What *system* is this animal a part of? What *color, number/quantity, or dimension* is associated with this animal?

continued

Table 2.1. *Common types of default questions* (continued)

Topic	Default Questions
Specific manmade object or type of manmade object (Rolls-Royce, expensive passenger automobile)	What *locations* are associated with this object? How is this object *used*? What *larger entity* is this object part of? What is the *process* for making this object? What does this object *look like*? What *value* is associated with this object? What *dangers* are associated with this object?
Specific manmade place or type of manmade place (Roman Colosseum, sports arena)	What *events* are associated with this place? What *people* are associated with this place? What *location* is associated with this place? What *actions* are performed at this place? What *larger entity* is this place part of? How is this place *developed*? What *value* is associated with this place? What *dangers* are associated with this place?
Natural occurring phenomenon or event or type of naturally occurring phenomenon or event (Mount St. Helens eruption, volcanic eruption)	What *places* are associated with this phenomenon? What *time period* is associated with this phenomenon? What *causes or consequences* are associated with this phenomenon? What *happened/happens* during this phenomenon?
Specific manmade phenomenon or event or type of manmade phenomenon or event (Macy's Thanksgiving Day Parade, holiday event)	What *people* are associated with this event? What *time period* or date is associated with this event? What *places* are associated with this event? What *causes or consequences* are associated with this event? What *happened* during this event? What *equipment* was used during this event? What *problems* were caused or solved by this event?
Specific manmade abstraction or type of manmade abstraction (linear function, function; love, emotion)	What are the features of this abstraction that distinguish it from other abstractions? What are the necessary conditions for this abstraction? What does this abstraction help explain or organize? What are some types of this abstraction? In what situations is this abstraction useful or important? Into what category does this abstraction fall?

Note: For a detailed discussion of these types of questions, see Marzano, Norford, and Ruyle (2019).

▶ Prior to receiving the information about the topic, the teacher asks students to answer the questions and explain why they think their answers are accurate.

▶ After experiencing the new information about the topic, the teacher asks students to reexamine their original answers in light of this new information.

▶ The teacher asks students to summarize what they have learned and how their thinking has changed.

To illustrate, consider the following task.

> While involved in a unit on the importance of monuments within a culture, the teacher has students watch a video about the Statue of Liberty. Before watching the video, the teacher asks students to respond to the following questions:
>
> - Where is the Statue of Liberty?
> - What does it look like?
> - How did the United States get the Statue of Liberty?
> - What does the Statue of Liberty symbolize?
>
> As students answer these questions, the teacher periodically asks them how they know their answers are accurate. Students watch the video and then discuss and reconsider their answers.

At the upper elementary and middle school levels, the task design process includes the following:

▶ The teacher identifies how students will receive information about the target topic.

▶ The teacher structures specific questions for students that will cue them to make default inferences.

▶ Prior to receiving information about the topic, the teacher asks students to answer the questions and to rate how sure they are about their answers.

▶ After students have received the information about the topic, the teacher asks them to reevaluate their original answers and their levels of confidence in their answers.

▶ The teacher asks students to summarize what they have learned and describe where their thinking has changed.

To illustrate, consider the following task.

A middle school dance teacher wishes to elicit default elaborations about underlying principles for the following two concepts of movement: alignment balance and weight shift. Prior to watching a video presentation on these movement concepts, the teacher has students respond to the following questions about the principles:

- As a dancer, what do you have to do to attain alignment balance and proper weight shift?
- What are the effects of achieving alignment balance?
- What are the effects of achieving weight shift?

After each question and answer, students use the following code to indicate how sure they are about their answers: completely sure (CS), mostly sure (MS), and slightly sure (SS). As some students read their answers aloud, the teacher asks them to explain why they assigned a particular confidence score. The teacher organizes students into small groups, where they share their answers and the explanations for their ratings.

Students then watch the video and reexamine the answer to the question. The teacher again has them work in small groups to describe the changes they wish to make in their answers and what led them to make those changes.

At the high school level, the task design process includes the following:

- The teacher identifies how students will receive information about the target topic.

- The teacher structures specific questions for students that will cue them to make default inferences.

- Prior to receiving the information about the topic, the teacher asks students to answer the questions and attach the qualifiers *all, most,* or *few* or the qualifiers *always, frequently, or seldom* to their answers.

- After students have received their information about the topic, the teacher asks them to reconsider the qualifiers they have used and determine any changes they see fit. If they make changes in the qualifiers they use, the teacher asks them to explain why.

- The teacher asks students to summarize what they have learned and describe how their thinking has changed.

To illustrate this process, consider the following task.

A high school teacher has students read general information about Democrats and Republicans. Prior to reading about them, the teacher asks students to answer the following questions about each:

- What general beliefs do Republicans have?
- What general beliefs do Democrats have?
- What noteworthy current events do you associate with Republicans?
- What noteworthy current events do you associate with Democrats?

The teacher directs students to add the following qualifiers to their answers: *all*, *most*, or *some* or *always*, *frequently*, or *seldom*. For example, one student might say that all Republicans believe in lowering taxes. Another student might say that most Republicans believe in lowering taxes, and still another student might say that some Republicans believe in lowering taxes.

After students have read the information provided by the teacher, students reexamine their qualifiers and discuss any changes they believe they should make in their answers or the qualifiers they applied to their answers.

Across the grade levels, default elaboration tasks require students to increasingly examine how sure they are about their inferences and the extent to which their inferences partially or completely apply to the new topic. This is particularly the case at the secondary level, where students are required to determine whether the characteristics they infer about particular topics (e.g., Republicans versus Democrats) apply to all examples of the topic or only to some. This gets to the heart of rigor because students are refining what they believe to be true about a topic in the context of comparing what they think is true and what they experience with new information about the topic.

Other ways to manipulate the difficulty of this cognitive analysis process include

- asking questions about more abstract and complex characteristics; and
- having students research the accuracy of their default elaborations.

Analyzing Errors (Common Errors in Reasoning)

As described in the Introduction, analyzing errors involves identifying common errors in reasoning or errors in the execution of a procedure. In effect, there are two types of the cognitive analysis processes relative to analyzing errors. One is applied to declarative knowledge and the other is applied to procedural knowledge. Here we focus on the one intended for declarative knowledge, which involves identifying common errors in reasoning.

To utilize error analysis with declarative knowledge, students must understand the various types of common errors in reasoning. In general, there are four types of common errors in reasoning:

- Errors in Faulty Logic: This type of error occurs when people form conclusions not supported by sound reasoning.

- Errors of Attack: This type of error occurs when people try to prove their point by disparaging or threating the counterposition.

- Errors of Weak Reference: This type of error occurs when people use information from untrustworthy or irrelevant sources to support their conclusions.

- Errors of Misinformation: This type of error occurs when people use incorrect information to support a conclusion.

Table 2.2 describes specific errors within each of these four types.

Students must know at least some of these types of errors before they can analyze errors rigorously. We consider how teachers should teach and provide practice in identifying these types of errors in Chapter 5. These errors should be presented to the students over time, with the more complex ones introduced at the high school level.

At the primary level, the design process for analyzing errors with declarative knowledge is as follows:

- The teacher identifies information about a specific topic that contains one or both of the following types of errors: poisoning the well and arguing against the person.

- The teacher isolates this content for students and asks them to identify the type of error it contains.

- The teacher asks students to summarize what they have learned and describe how their thinking has changed.

Table 2.2. *Common errors in reasoning*

Errors of Faulty Logic

Contradiction: Presenting conflicting information to support a claim.

Accident: Failing to recognize that your evidence is based on an exception to a rule.

False Cause: Confusing a temporal (time) relationship between events with a causal relationship.

Begging the Question: Making a claim and then supporting it with similar statements that do not constitute evidence.

Evading the Issue: Sidestepping an issue by changing the topic.

Arguing from Ignorance: Supporting a claim simply because its opposite cannot be proven.

Composition/Division: Asserting that something is true about the whole because it is true about one of the parts (composition), or asserting that something is true about a part because it is associated with the whole (division).

Errors of Attack

Poisoning the Well: Attacking everything that is offered in opposition to your own position.

Arguing Against the Person: Making derogatory comments about anyone who is arguing against your position.

Appealing the Force: Threatening to psychologically or physically harm anyone who is arguing against your position.

Errors of Weak References

Using Sources That Reflect Bias: Referencing sources that contain habitual bias or confirmatory bias.

Using Sources That Lack Credibility: Using sources that have no documented record of being knowledgeable about a topic or who are known for providing inaccurate information.

Appealing to Authority: Relying on one's superior status (e.g., socially, corporately) as the evidence that your claim is true.

Appealing to the People: Asserting that your claim is true because it is a popular position.

Appealing to Emotion: Eliciting emotion in support of your claim as the primary evidence that it is true.

Errors of Misinformation

Confusing the Facts: Distorting or modifying facts to support your claim.

Misapplying a Concept for Generalization: Using inaccurate information about a concept or generalization to support your claim.

To illustrate how this process might look in the classroom, consider the following task.

> In a unit on weather, the teacher has introduced the topic of climate change. Previously, the teacher exposed students to the reasoning errors of poisoning the well and arguing against the person. The teacher tells students that most people agree that the climate is changing, but they don't agree as to why it's changing.
>
> The teacher presents three video segments: one that exemplifies poisoning the well, one that exemplifies arguing against the person, and one that doesn't contain any examples of errors In reasoning The teacher plays each recording for students and asks them to determine whether it demonstrates an error in reasoning, and if it does, which of the two types it exemplifies.

At the upper elementary level and middle school level, the teacher expands the type of reasoning errors students are expected to know. Additionally, the teacher does not isolate statements for students. The task design process at the upper elementary and middle school levels includes the following:

- The teacher provides students with specific information about a topic.
- The teacher has students look for and identify the following types of errors in the information about the topic: appealing to force, appealing to authority, appealing to the people, and appealing to emotion, in addition to poisoning of the well and arguing against the person.
- The teacher asks students to summarize what they have learned and describe how their thinking has changed.

To illustrate the process consider the following tasks.

> During a unit on the US Constitution, the teacher has introduced the topic that some US citizens believe the Constitution should be dramatically changed in certain areas, whereas others say it should not be changed. The teacher has identified three specific sources on the Internet. She asks students to identify specific errors in reasoning in each of these sources and then determine which sources had the most errors and which had the fewest errors.

At the secondary level, students are expected to recognize the full spectrum of errors from all categories. Students are also expected to identify sources on their own as opposed to only those provided by the teacher and analyze their sources for errors in reasoning. The task design process at the high school level includes the following:

▶ The teacher provides students with a topic for which people hold differing opinions.

▶ The teacher has students identify multiple sources about the topic and analyze those sources for the various types of reasoning errors.

▶ The teacher has students determine the extent to which the identified errors affect the credibility of the sources.

▶ The teacher asks students to summarize what they have learned and describe how their thinking has changed.

To illustrate this process, consider the following task.

> The teacher has introduced the topic of gun control and its relationship to the Second Amendment. The teacher has students identify at least three sources on this topic and then analyze each source for errors in reasoning. Each student then describes in writing the extent to which the identified errors affect the validity and credibility of each source.

Across the grade levels, students are expected to identify an increasingly larger array of errors. Students are also asked to increasingly judge the overall quality of a source based on the number and types of reasoning errors it has.

Other than task design, the difficulty of tasks involving analyzing errors can be manipulated by

▶ having students correct errors they find in sources; and

▶ having students rate various sources in terms of the number of errors they typically include.

Habits of Mind

There are two habits of mind that are particularly relevant when initially learning about declarative knowledge: seeking clarity and seeking accuracy.

Seeking Clarity

The disposition of seeking clarity involves students being aware when they are not clear about specific information and then doing something to rectify the situation. A process for seeking clarity the teacher might present to the students includes the following:

- Identify if something is unclear to you.
- Identify a question you need to ask for the information to become more clear.
- Ask your question and seek the answer.

At first, the teacher should walk students through the process. For example, when students are receiving information that they compare with their default elaborations, the teacher might ask students to stop for a moment and determine if there is any part of the information about which they are unclear. She would then guide them in forming questions about specific points of confusion. The teacher then organizes students into groups that share the same questions. Students in groups then use Internet sources to answer their clarifying questions.

As students become more skilled at using the process by themselves, the teacher occasionally has students rate themselves using the following scale:

4. I've been seeking clarity without any teacher reminders.
3. I've been aware of when I'm not seeking clarity, but I still don't do a good job of trying to do so.
2. I've been trying to seek clarity when the teacher reminds me, but not otherwise.
1. I really haven't been trying to seek clarity.

Seeking Accuracy

The habit of mind of seeking accuracy involves identifying situations for which you conclude that you need to be accurate and taking steps to do so. The teacher might cue students to use this disposition by providing them with the following steps:

- Identify a specific topic about which you believe it is important to be accurate.
- Identify sources you might use.
- Consult your sources and try to describe any previous misconceptions you had about the topic.

While students engage in tasks involving analyzing errors, the teacher might ask them to identify conclusions the accuracy of which they are unsure. This might involve information cited in a source that they think is incorrect. The teacher would then provide time for students to check the accuracy of their conclusions and report on what they found.

Occasionally, but systematically, the teacher asks students to evaluate themselves using the following scale:

4. I've been seeking accuracy without any teacher reminders.
3. I've been aware of when I'm not seeking accuracy, but I still don't do a good job of trying to do so.
2. I've been trying to seek accuracy when the teacher reminds me, but not otherwise.
1. I really haven't been trying to seek accuracy.

Cognitive Analysis Questions

The two cognitive analysis processes addressed in this chapter are default elaborations and analyzing common errors in reasoning. Both processes are particularly applicable to declarative knowledge.

Questions that might be used with tasks involving default elaborations include:

- What are some characteristics of your default elaborations you were not aware of?
- What are some characteristics of the topic you made default elaborations about that you were not aware of?
- What was the most difficult part of analyzing your default elaborations? Why?

Questions that might be used with tasks focusing on common errors in reasoning include:

- What are some characteristics of the errors you found that you were not aware of?
- What are some characteristics of the topic you are studying that you were not aware of?
- What was the most difficult part of identifying errors? Why?

Habits of Mind Questions

The two habits of mind that fit particularly well with learning declarative knowledge are seeking clarity and seeking accuracy.

Questions that might be used with seeking clarity include:

- What things do you become aware of that let you know you should be seeking clarity?
- When you are unclear about something, what emotions do you feel and what do you say to yourself?
- What's one small thing you could do to get better at seeking clarity?

Questions that might be used with seeking accuracy include:

- What things do you become aware of that let you know you should be seeking accuracy?
- When you know you are not being accurate, what emotions do you feel and what do you say to yourself?
- What is one small thing you could do to get better at seeking accuracy?

Summary

This chapter addressed enhancing rigor when initially learning declarative knowledge. When students are initially learning declarative knowledge, it is important to remember that teachers should first identify a small set of topics on which to focus before planning tasks. Cognitive analysis tasks that are particularly suited to enhancing rigor in this situation include default elaborations and analyzing common errors in reasoning. These tasks become more abstract, more complex, and more student directed as they progress through the grade levels. Specific habits of mind can also be taught and reinforced in the context of cognitive analysis tasks. The chapter addressed how the disposition of seeking clarity and the disposition of seeking accuracy should be employed in such tasks.

CHAPTER 3

Rigor with Procedural Knowledge

By its very nature, procedural knowledge involves generating something new. Stated differently, when a procedure is executed, something is made explicit that was not explicit before. When you execute the procedure of adding numbers like 45, 78, and 3, you get a sum that was not explicit before the procedure was executed—in this case, 126. When you execute the procedure of writing a friendly letter, something new is produced—the letter to your friend. When you execute the procedure of scrambling two eggs, something new is produced—breakfast.

We saw in Chapter 1 that procedural knowledge is not as plentiful as declarative knowledge when it comes to standards in K–12 education. However, the procedures that are found in the standards are typically considered the centerpiece of their subject areas. For example, the standards within history are overwhelmingly declarative, but the relatively few procedures like conducting a historical investigation are prominent within the recommended history curriculum. Table 3.1 provides some examples of procedures important to various subject areas.

Table 3.1. *Examples of procedures within various subject areas*

Subject Area	Sample Procedural Knowledge
Mathematics	Solving linear equations
Language Arts Reading	Sounding out an unrecognized word while reading
Language Arts Writing	Writing a descriptive essay
Foreign Language	Using common idioms in informal conversation
Geography	Reading a contour map
Health	Employing a personal exercise routine
Physical Education	Throwing and catching a ball
Arts – Music	Playing the scale on a violin
Technology – Coding	Troubleshooting a set of code with errors

Procedures come in many forms. Some of them are relatively short and straightforward, like reading a bar graph. It involves a few steps that can be executed in a relatively short period of time. Some procedures are quite long and involve embedded subprocedures, and are referred to as complex procedures. For example, creating a video presentation is a complex procedure with embedded subprocedures. You must identify the content that will be in the presentation and script it. This, in itself, requires multiple drafts and editing. You must create a storyboard indicating the various scenes in the presentation, and then record those shots, and so on.

As is the case with declarative knowledge, one of the first jobs of the teacher is to determine what procedures will be the focus for enhancing rigor. As is the case with declarative knowledge, rigor can be enhanced when students are first learning procedural knowledge and after they have acquired an initial familiarity with it. In this chapter, we consider enhancing procedural knowledge after students have initially learned it.

Cognitive Analysis Processes

There are two cognitive analysis processes that apply well to procedural knowledge to which students have already been introduced: comparing and classifying.

Comparing

As is the case with declarative knowledge, the cognitive analysis process of comparing can enhance the rigor with which students execute procedural knowledge. Again, the process involves the identification of increasingly more complex characteristics. At the primary level, the task design process includes the following:

▸ The teacher identifies the procedures to be compared.

▸ The teacher identifies simple characteristics on which to compare the procedures.

▸ The teacher asks students to describe how the procedures are similar and/or different.

▸ The teacher asks students to summarize what they have learned and how their thinking has changed.

To illustrate this process, consider the following task.

> The teacher has been working on word problems that involve an additive relationship and word problems that involve a multiplicative relationship. The teacher asks students to compare problems with additive relationships with problems that involve multiplicative relationships in terms of the words and phrases that signal each type of relationship. To accomplish this, students examine the practice problems they have been doing.

At the upper elementary and middle school levels, the teacher uses the same design process but focuses on more complex or abstract characteristics on which to compare the procedures. The task design process at the upper elementary and middle school level includes the following:

- The teacher identifies the procedures to be compared.
- The teacher identifies complex or abstract characteristics on which to compare the procedures.
- The teacher asks students to describe how the procedures are similar and/or different.
- The teacher asks students to summarize what they have learned and explain how their thinking has changed.

To illustrate this process, consider the following task.

> Students have been working on writing narrative and expository essays. The teacher asks them to compare how their overall structures are similar and different in terms of
>
> - how they begin and end;
> - the progression of information between where they begin and where they end; and
> - how their different structures affect the writing process.

At the high school level, the teacher identifies the items to be compared and asks students to identify the complex or abstract characteristics on which to compare them and justify why those characteristics are important. More specifically, at the high school level, the task design process includes the following:

- The teacher identifies the procedures to be compared.
- The teacher asks students to identify complex or abstract characteristics on which to compare the procedures and justify why those characteristics are important to understanding the procedures.

▸ The teacher asks students to describe how the procedures are similar and/or different.

▸ The teacher asks students to summarize what they have learned and describe how their thinking has changed.

To illustrate this process, consider the following task.

Students have been studying the procedures for conducting an exploratory study on the effects of a specific intervention and a confirmatory study on the effects of a specific type of intervention. Students are asked to identify at least two characteristics on which to compare these procedures and justify why their characteristics are important to both procedures. Students then describe how the procedures are similar and/or different on the selected characteristics.

As with declarative knowledge, comparing tasks with procedural knowledge progresses in difficulty across the grade levels by employing more abstract and complex characteristics and by turning over control of the task design process to students.

There are a number of other ways to manipulate the complexity of comparing tasks for procedural knowledge, including

▸ using more than two procedures; and

▸ increasing the number of characteristics on which procedures are compared.

Classifying

The cognitive analysis processes of subordinate classifying and superordinate classifying apply both to procedural knowledge and to declarative knowledge.

Subordinate Classifying

Subordinate classifying involves identifying the various types of or categories within a given procedure. At the primary level, the task design process includes the following:

▸ The teacher identifies the procedure on which to focus.

▸ The teacher identifies the subcategories within the procedure.

▸ The teacher presents students with items that fit into the subcategories.

▸ The teacher asks students to sort the items into the identified subcategories.

▸ The teacher asks students to summarize what they have learned and describe how their thinking has changed.

To illustrate, consider the following task.

> Students have been working on word problems that involve division. The teacher presents them with two categories: division problems that involve remainders and division problems that do not involve remainders. Students are provided with ten division word problems and are asked to sort them into these two categories.

At the upper elementary and middle school levels, the teacher identifies the procedure on which to focus but provides students with some control over the subcategories. The task design process at this level includes the following:

- The teacher identifies the procedure on which to focus.
- The teacher provides students with some of the subcategories and asks students to identify at least one other subcategory.
- The teacher asks students to identify items that fit into the subcategories and defend their choices.
- The teacher asks students to summarize what they have learned and describe how their thinking has changed.

To illustrate, consider the following task.

> In a middle school mathematics class, students have been working on a variety of multistep word problems. The teacher explains that one type of multistep problem they have been doing involves adding first and multiplying second. The teacher asks students to describe at least one other type of multistep problem along with examples of that type.

Finally, at the high school level, the task design process includes the following:

- The teacher or students identify the procedure on which to focus.
- The teacher asks students to identify subcategories for procedures with the provision that some categories are ones that are new and unique.
- The teacher asks students to identify procedures that fit into the new subcategories and defend their choices.
- The teacher asks students to summarize what they have learned and how their thinking has changed.

To illustrate, consider the following task.

> Students have been studying three basic types of mathematical proofs: direct proofs, proofs by contradiction, and proofs by induction. The teacher asks students to create a unique category of proofs that might share characteristics of the types of proofs they have been studying. Students are to describe the defining characteristics of their new category and provide at least two examples of proofs that fit into this new category.

Across the grade levels, subordinate classifying becomes more complex as characteristics become more complex and abstract. Additionally, students have more control over the task design process as they progress through the grade levels. Other ways to manipulate the difficulty of subordinate classification tasks include

- increasing the number of subcategories in the task; and
- using multiple levels of subcategories.

Superordinate Classifying

Superordinate classifying involves identifying the category into which a procedure can be classified. Again, at the primary level, tasks would have to be highly structured by the teacher. The task design process at this level includes the following:

- The teacher identifies the superordinate category into which a procedure belongs.
- The teacher identifies the characteristics of that superordinate category.
- The teacher asks students to describe how the characteristics of the superordinate category apply to the procedure.
- The teacher asks students to summarize what they have learned and describe how their thinking has changed.

To illustrate, consider the following task.

> Students have been creating tally charts to record data. The teacher explains that this is a type of graph and that graphs have the following characteristics:
>
> - a title that describes what's in the graph;
> - two or more things that are represented; and
> - a way to label or assign numbers to the two or more things.
>
> The teacher then asks students to describe how those characteristics look in a tally chart.

At the upper elementary and middle school levels, students have more input in the task. To accomplish this, the task design process includes the following:

- The teacher identifies the procedure and the superordinate category to which it belongs.
- The teacher asks students to describe the characteristics of that superordinate category.
- The teacher asks students to describe how the characteristics of the superordinate category manifest in the procedure.
- The teacher asks students to summarize what they have learned and describe how their thinking has changed.

To illustrate, consider the following task.

> In a language arts class, students have been given a process for ensuring that their essays are clear and have an overall logic. The teacher reminds them that what they are doing is a type of editing procedure. The teacher asks students to describe some of the characteristics of effective editing procedures in general and explain how the characteristics apply to the process of ensuring that their essays have an overall logic.

At the high school level, students have a great deal of latitude within the task. The task design process at this level includes the following:

- The teacher identifies two or more categories into which the procedure belongs.
- The teacher asks students to articulate the defining characteristics of each of the categories.
- The teacher asks students to describe how each classification provides a unique perspective on the procedure.
- The teacher asks students to summarize what they have learned and describe how their thinking has changed.

To illustrate, consider the following task:

> In an art class, students have been using a unique brush stroke procedure designed by the teacher. The teacher explains that what they have been doing could be thought of as a hatching procedure or a drybrush procedure. The teacher asks them to describe the defining characteristics of each procedure and how the characteristics of each can be found in the new procedure created by the teacher.

Again, across the grade levels, superordinate categories become more sophisticated and students exert more control over the process.

Ways to further manipulate the difficulty of superordinate classifying tasks include

- increasing the number of superordinate categories; and
- using multiple levels of superordinate categories.

Habits of Mind

Two habits of mind fit particularly well with procedural knowledge: developing fluency and seeking cohesion and coherence.

Developing Fluency

Fluency is specific to procedural knowledge and involves working quickly and accurately. This requires a fine balance of attending to speed while ensuring that mistakes are not made. To foster this disposition, a teacher must structure practice sessions in a way that emphasizes how quickly as well as how accurately a procedure is being executed. The classic example of this is keyboarding. The ideal level of expertise relative to keyboarding is that students can perform it quickly and without error. The following process can be presented to students as an aid to developing fluency:

- Before you start the process, focus your attention on trying to work as quickly as you can without making errors.
- As you work, occasionally stop and ask yourself if you are moving quickly enough and not letting yourself get bogged down.
- As you work, occasionally stop and ask yourself if you're paying attention to avoid mistakes.

When initially introducing this process, the teacher would use highly structured practice sessions. For example, the teacher might design practice sessions to help students develop fluency relative to the process of determining the main idea of an expository passage. The teacher would start with relatively short passages and remind students that as they read, they should strive for a balance of speed and accuracy. As students are reading the structural passages, the teacher occasionally stops them and reminds them to keep their speed up and not get too caught up in the details. Also, the teacher occasionally reminds students to read quickly but not so quickly that they are starting to make mistakes. When students are finished, the teacher leads a discussion about the difficulties of trying to balance speed and accuracy. The teacher reminds students that when seeking fluency, you are always making adjustments to either move more quickly or pay more attention to accuracy. As students become more independent at fluency, the teacher occasionally has them rate themselves using the following scale:

4. I've been seeking fluency without any teacher reminders.

3. I've been aware of when I should be seeking fluency, but I still don't do a good job of trying to do so.

2. I've been trying to seek fluency when the teacher reminds me, but not otherwise.

1. I really haven't been trying to seek fluency.

Seeking Cohesion and Coherence

The habit of mind of seeking cohesion and coherence involves ensuring that all the pieces and parts of a complex process fit together to form a unified whole. Relative to procedural knowledge, the teacher can present students with the following process for seeking cohesion and coherence:

▸ Identify what part of the procedure you are working on right now.

▸ Determine whether what you are doing with this part is working against what you did in another part of the process.

▸ If so, identify what changes you have to make to ensure that all parts of the process are working together.

By definition, seeking cohesion and coherence is most compatible with complex processes that involve a number of embedded subprocesses. For example, a teacher might have students practice the disposition of seeking cohesion and coherence with the complex process of editing a composition. The teacher would begin by explaining the nature and importance of seeking cohesion and coherence. The teacher would then provide students with an essay to edit and remind them that, while editing, they should be considering multiple aspects of the essay, including overall structure, subject-verb agreement, punctuation, and word choice. As students are editing the essay, the teacher would periodically ask them to stop and consider how the part of the editing process they are currently working on interacts with the other parts of the editing process.

Over time, the teacher would have students rate themselves using the following scale:

4. I've been seeking cohesion and coherence without any teacher reminders.

3. I've been aware of when I should be seeking cohesion and coherence, but I still don't do a good job of trying to do so.

2. I've been trying to seek cohesion and coherence when the teacher reminds me, but not otherwise.

1. I really haven't been trying to seek cohesion and coherence.

Cognitive Analysis Questions

The cognitive analysis processes addressed in this chapter are comparing, subordinate classifying, and superordinate classifying. They apply to procedural knowledge as well as they do to declarative knowledge.

Questions that might be used with comparing tasks include:

- What are some similarities in these procedures you were unaware of?
- What are some differences in these procedures you were unaware of?
- Which were harder to identify: similarities or differences? Why?

Questions that might be used with subordinate classifying tasks include:

- What are some subcategories within this procedure you were not aware of?
- What are some characteristics of this procedure you were not aware of?
- What was most difficult about identifying subcategories? Why?

Questions that might be used with superordinate classifying include:

- What are some of the superordinate categories for this procedure you were not aware of?
- What are some characteristics of this procedure you were not aware of?
- What was most difficult about identifying superordinate categories? Why?

Habits of Mind Questions

The two habits of mind that fit particularly well with procedural knowledge are developing fluency and seeking cohesion and coherence.

Questions that might be used with developing fluency include:

- What things do you become aware of that let you know you should be developing fluency?
- When you know you're having difficulty with fluency, what emotions do you feel and what do you say to yourself?
- What is one small thing you could do to get better at developing fluency?

Questions that might be used with seeking cohesion and coherence include:

- What things do you become aware of that let you know you should be seeking cohesion and coherence?
- When you know you are having a problem with cohesion and coherence, what emotions do you feel and what do you say to yourself?
- What's one small thing you could do to get better at seeking cohesion and coherence?

Summary

This chapter addressed enhancing rigor with procedural knowledge after students have initially learned it. Procedures can be relatively short and straightforward or complex with embedded subprocedures. It is important that teachers identify specific procedures on which to focus, just as it is important that teachers identify specific topics within declarative knowledge on which to focus when designing tasks to enhance rigor. Cognitive analysis tasks that are particularly suited to enhancing rigor with procedural knowledge include comparing, subordinate classifying, and superordinate classifying. Habits of mind that are particularly amenable to procedural knowledge include developing fluency and seeking cohesion and coherence.

CHAPTER 4

Rigor When Initially Learning Procedural Knowledge

To a certain extent, learning procedural knowledge is more complex than learning declarative knowledge simply because it involves executing the steps in a procedure. As we saw in the last chapter, the steps of a procedure should be executed with fluency and in a manner that maintains cohesion and coherence relative to the product of the procedure. In effect, there are a lot working parts involved in learning a new procedure.

Without a doubt, the most important part of teaching a new procedure to students is to provide them with a clear vision of the steps that are involved. More pointedly, over the years, I have come to believe that the most effective teachers are quite skilled at proceduralizing content.

The Power of Proceduralizing

Although the term *proceduralizing* is not part of everyday vernacular, it should be an important part of teaching vernacular. Proceduralizing simply means creating a set of steps for vaguely defined processes. For example, if a company does not have a precise process in place for hiring new employees, it can increase the effectiveness of its hiring by creating an explicit procedure for doing so. Likewise, if a teacher is having a difficult time helping students increase their ability to read poems, he or she can create an explicit procedure for reading poems. I firmly believe that such procedures should initially be presented to students as step-by-step processes.

Step-by-Step Processes

Creating step-by-step processes is one of the most powerful instructional tools at a teacher's discretion. Once you become aware of the power of step-by-step processes, you start to see them everywhere. Indeed, step-by-step processes have been developed for a wide variety of purposes and fields. For example, there are websites devoted to proceduralizing academic and nonacademic content. To illustrate, wikiHow.com lists step-by-step processes for procedures ranging from baking a cake to giving a speech.

In effect, the good news for teachers is that educators have already created step-by-step processes for a great many of the procedures one might find in a K–12 curriculum. Teachers simply need to do an Internet search to find teacher-designed procedures that could be the focus of instruction.

Step-by-step processes come in a variety of forms. Some are relatively general, like the following step-by-step process for reading a poem:

1. Look over the poem and find the words you don't understand.
2. Look up those words in the dictionary.
3. Read the poem at least two or three times.
4. Ask yourself who the speaker is in the poem. (Hint: it might not be the poet.)
5. Say the poem in your own words. Do this stanza by stanza.
6. Summarize what the poem means in a few sentences.

Whereas some step-by-step processes are for general procedures, like reading a poem, others are for very specific procedures. The following is a specific process for sounding out an unrecognized one-syllable word when reading:

1. Identify the vowel sounds in the word.
2. Identify the ending sound and blend it with the vowel sound.
3. Identify the beginning sound in the word and blend it with the vowel sound and the ending sound.

Depending on how much direction a teacher wants to provide to students, step-by-step processes can be highly detailed. To illustrate, consider the following step-by-step process (adapted from We All Can Read, n.d.), which is also about sounding out unrecognized one-syllable words while reading.

Step 1: Identify the vowel sound.

Step 2: After identifying that vowel sound, identify the consonant sound that immediately follows the vowel sound.

Step 3: Blend together the vowel sound with the following consonant sound.

Step 4: If two consonants follow the vowel and can't be easily blended, then:

   ▸ Isolate the vowel sound and blend it with the first following consonant.

   ▸ Isolate the sound of the second consonant and blend it with the sound of the vowel and the first consonant.

Step 5: Next, identify the sound of the consonant letter that comes immediately before the vowel and blend it with the sound of the vowel and the other letters that come after the vowel.

Step 6: If two or three letters come before the vowel, determine if they form a team that make a recognizable sound and blend that sound with the sound of the vowel and the letter or letters that come after the vowel.

Step 7: If two or three consonant letters come before the vowel and don't make a team, start with the consonant nearest the vowel. Identify the sound of the consonant and blend it with the sound of the vowel and the letter or letters that come after the vowel. Then, identify the sound of the next adjacent consonant and blend it with the rest of the word that has already been decided. Do the same if there is a third consonant before the vowel.

Creating step-by-step processes should be one of the first steps a teacher takes when preparing to teach a new procedure simply because they provide students with a clear picture of what they are expected to do. I believe this is not only important, but also necessary even though it is somewhat artificial. That is, once we learn a procedure, we typically do not execute it as a series of rigid steps performed in a specific way. Indeed, as we learn procedures, we combine steps and commonly develop shorthand versions of the procedure. But in the beginning, a step-by-step process helps us view the new procedure as a concrete set of actions.

Once a step-by-step procedure has been constructed, it is easy to create worked examples.

Worked Examples

Knowledge that has been proceduralized can be turned into worked examples by adding illustrations of key steps. To illustrate, consider the following worked example for constructing a histogram:

Step 1: Gather the data you want to graph: A histogram will depict the frequency of the data. For example, assume you wanted to examine the frequency of scores received by students on a test. You find that those scores are 98, 77, 76, 74, 67, 90, 94, 92, 83, 79, 79, 72, 71, 78, 78, 75, 99, 85, 85, 88, 73, 70, 68, 65, 86, 89, 84, 84, 80, 83, 89, 82, 83, 80, and 80.

Step 2: Identify the range of your categories or bins: To make your histogram easy to read, you can define categories or bins into which you will sort the data. In this case, the following bins could be useful:

100–95

94–90

89–85

84–80

79–75

74–70

69–65

Step 3: Sort the data into the bins: Identify which bin each data point fits into. For example, consider the bin 100–95, which has the following scores in it: 98 and 99. The bin 79–75 has the following scores in it: 79, 78, 79, 79, 78, 78, 75, and 75.

Step 4: Count the number of data points in each bin: In this case, if the bins have the following frequencies:

Bin	Number of Data Points (Frequencies)
100–95	2
94–90	3
89–85	6
84–80	9
79–75	8
74–70	5
69–65	3

Step 5: Draw and label the axes of your histogram: Each histogram has two axes: an x axis and a y axis. The x axis represents the bins. The y axis represents the frequencies.

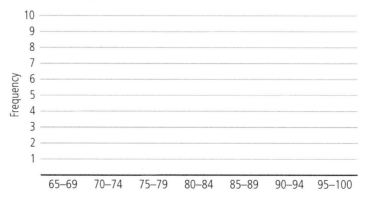

Step 6: Draw the bars on your histogram: Draw a bar representing each bin. The top of each bar should stop at the point that represents the frequency for each bin.

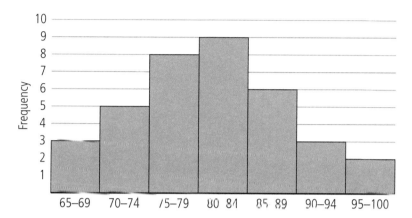

A worked example, then, is a step-by-step process with specific examples that illustrate key steps. Worked examples provide students with clear exemplars of what a procedure looks like when it is executed properly.

Once step-by-step processes have been designed and include accompanying worked examples, a teacher has made the necessary preparations to enhance rigor when students are first learning procedural knowledge.

Using The Cognitive Analysis Processes

There are two cognitive analysis processes that work well as tools for enhancing rigor when students are initially learning procedural knowledge: analyzing errors and elaborating.

Analyzing Errors (Identifying "Bugs")

Analyzing errors with procedural knowledge is different from analyzing errors with declarative knowledge. When applied to declarative knowledge, analyzing errors involves looking for common errors in reasoning. These were discussed in depth in Chapter 2. When applied to procedural knowledge analyzing errors involves looking for errors or "bugs" in a procedure. The term bugs is actually a technical one relative to procedural knowledge. The National Research Council (2004) describe bugs as in the following example:

> When students attempt to apply conventional algorithms without conceptually grasping why and how the algorithm works, "bugs" are sometimes introduced.

For example, teachers have long wrestled with the frequent difficulties that second and third graders have with multidigit subtraction in problems such as:

$$\begin{array}{r} 51 \\ -14 \\ \hline \end{array}$$

A common error is:

$$\begin{array}{r} 51 \\ -14 \\ \hline 43 \end{array}$$

These "buggy algorithms" are often both resilient and persistent. Consider how reasonable the above procedure is: in addition problems that look similar, children can add up or down and get a correct result either way:

$$\begin{array}{r} 51 \\ +14 \\ \hline 65 \end{array}$$

Bugs often remain undetected when teachers do not see the highly regular pattern in students' errors, responding to them more as though they were random miscalculations. (p. 69)

This subtraction procedure is a classic case in which children subtract "up" when they find subtracting "down" is not possible. Here, students would try to subtract four from one and, seeing that they could not do this, would subtract one from four instead. In this chapter, I use the term *bugs* to refer to steps that are left out of a procedure or that aren't executed correctly. Therefore, analyzing errors when first learning procedural knowledge is tantamount to helping students identify the bugs they might be unknowingly and inadvertently inserting into procedures they are learning.

The teacher should begin by providing students with a step-by-step process he or she has designed. The teacher demonstrates the steps and provides some initial practice using the steps. After students have a general idea as to how the steps are executed, the teacher then engages students in tasks designed to help them detect possible bugs in their procedure.

At the primary level, the task design process includes the following:

- The teacher reviews with students the step-by-step process for a procedure they have been learning.

- The teacher provides students with a short task that requires them to use the step-by-step process.

- Next, the teacher provides students with a worked example of the procedure or part of the procedure.

- The teacher then has students compare the steps they used with the steps used in the worked example of the task and identify anything they did differently from the worked example.

- If students did something differently, the teacher leads a discussion as to whether that difference represented an error or simply a different way to execute the procedure.

- The teacher asks students to summarize what they have learned and describe how their thinking has changed.

To illustrate, consider the following task.

> The teacher has provided students with a step-by-step process to sound out an unrecognized word while reading. The teacher reviews the process with students and then provides them with one or two words to sound out. The teacher then provides them with a video recording of himself using the step-by-step process after the students have tried sounding out the practice words. This video represents a worked example for students. The teacher asks students to carefully examine the worked example to identify differences in how he sounded out the words and how they did it. If students find differences, they discuss them as a class to determine the difference responds errors.

It is important to note that some students will find no errors when they compare the process they use and that which was provided in the worked example. This is fine; these students will still benefit because of the deep level of analysis in which they have been engaged.

At the upper elementary level and middle school level, the task design process includes the following:

- The teacher reviews the step-by-step process for a procedure students have been learning.

- The teacher provides students with a short task that requires them to use the process.

- ‣ The teacher provides students with a worked example of the process.
- ‣ The teacher then has students compare how they executed the task and the worked example of the task.
- ‣ The teacher asks students to identify parts of the process they used to identify steps they might change based on what they observed in the worked example.
- ‣ The students then describe their new procedure with the changes they have made.
- ‣ The teacher asks students to summarize what they have learned and describe how their thinking has changed.

To illustrate, consider the following task.

A middle school science teacher has provided students with a step-by-step process for conducting a lab experiment in a manner that is both safe and precise. The teacher has students set up a brief lab experiment and then compares the steps they used with a worked example of the step-by-step process the teacher has created. Students examine the steps they used with the ones in the worked example. As students find differences, they determine what type of changes they need to make in their process. Students then describe and discuss the changes they made.

At the high school level, the design process includes the following:

- ‣ The teacher provides students with a step-by-step process for a subprocedure within a complex procedure.
- ‣ The teacher provides students with a worked example of the subprocedure.
- ‣ The teacher then has students compare how they executed the task and the worked example of the task.
- ‣ The teacher asks students to identify parts of their personal subprocedures that they might change based on what they observed in the worked example.
- ‣ The students then describe their new procedure with the changes they have made.
- ‣ Students also describe how their new subprocedure will influence the larger, more complex procedure in which it is embedded.
- ‣ The teacher asks students to summarize what they have learned and describe how their thinking has changed.

Here the task design focuses on a subprocedure embedded in a more complex procedure and requires students to consider how changes they might make in the subprocedure may affect the overall complex procedure. To illustrate, consider the following task.

> Students are provided a step-by-step process for editing a composition for subject-verb agreement, which is embedded in a much larger procedure of editing for multiple factors such as word choice, transitions, and overall logic. Students are also provided with a worked example that they compare with steps they personally use. They make changes in their personal procedures and consider how the subprocedure influences that larger procedure into which it is embedded. Some students find that being more efficient at the subprocedure of editing for subject-verb agreement makes the overall editing process much more cohesive and coherent. Some students don't find any errors in their subprocedures but still benefit from this deep level of analysis of the editing process.

Across the grade levels, analyzing errors for procedural knowledge becomes more complex starting with students simply noting differences between a worked example and the process they use and moving to examining changes they should make in a subprocedure of a complex procedure.

Some other ways to manipulate the complexity of analyzing errors for procedural knowledge include

- having students look for errors in multiple steps; and
- having students describe the probable consequences of the errors they find.

Elaborating (Reasoned Elaborations; If/Then)

In previous chapters, we saw that there are two types of elaborations or inferences: default and reasoned. We discussed default elaborations in Chapter 2 when initially learning declarative knowledge. The second type of elaboration involves reasoned inferences. With this type of inference, we use "if/then" thinking: if this is true, then something else should be true. This type of elaboration involves experimentation and is useful for enhancing rigor relative to procedural knowledge.

As described previously, when first teaching procedural knowledge, the teacher begins with a clear step-by-step process and provides some introductory experiences with the procedure. These experiences might include activities for identifying errors ("bugs") as described previously.

Worked examples are necessary for students to identify errors in procedures. However, worked examples are not necessary for students to engage in reasoned elaborations. Asking students to engage in reasoned elaboration should take place after students have had some initial experiences with a new procedure.

At the primary level, the task design process for reasoned elaboration tasks includes the following:

▶ The teacher focuses students' attention on the step-by-step process to which they have already been introduced.

▶ The teacher selects one (or more) steps in the step-by-step process and asks students to describe what is easy for them and what is hard for them regarding the step or steps.

▶ The teacher asks students to describe how the step or steps could be made easier for them.

▶ The teacher has students try out their ideas.

▶ The teacher has students summarize what they have learned and discuss how their thinking has changed.

To illustrate, consider the following task.

> The teacher has provided students with a step-by-step process for sounding out an unrecognized one-syllable word. That process focuses first on the vowel, which is then blended with the ending sounds, and finally blended with the beginning sounds. As a whole class guided by the teacher, students talk about which part of the process they find most difficult or confusing. The teacher leads the class in a discussion of how they might make the process clearer. The students then try out the new process and discuss how the changes make the process easier.

At the upper elementary and middle school levels, the task design process includes the following:

▶ The teacher focuses students' attention on the step-by-step process to which they have already been introduced.

▶ The teacher guides the students as a whole group or in small groups in selecting one or more steps in the procedure and changing them to make it more effective.

- The teacher asks students to generate hypotheses about the changes the altered step(s) will create.
- The teacher has students execute the altered process to test out their hypotheses.
- The teacher has students summarize what they have learned and discuss how their thinking has changed about the procedure.

At this level, the teacher turns over part of the design process to small groups of students—most noteworthy, the identification of what step or steps will be changed.

To illustrate, consider the following task:

A middle school mathematics teacher has provided students with a step-by-step process for designing box and whisker plots. After reviewing the process, the teacher leads the whole class in a discussion of how changes in the process might or might not affect the efficiency and accuracy of the process. As a whole group, the class decides to make some changes to what appear to be two key steps. They try out the altered process and discuss the results.

At the high school level, the task design process includes the following:

- The teacher focuses students' attention on the step-by-step process to which they have already been introduced.
- The teacher asks students to individually select one (or more) critical steps in the procedure to change and the manner in which it will be changed.
- The teacher asks students to individually generate hypotheses about the changes the altered step(s) will create.
- The teacher has students execute their altered process to test out their hypotheses.
- The teacher has students summarize what they have learned and discuss how their thinking has changed about the procedure.

At the high school level, the students individually identify what they will change in the process and hypothesize what will change.

To illustrate this design process, consider the following task:

A chemistry teacher has created a step-by-step process for balancing chemical equations. That process has students:

- Identify elements
- Determine net charge on each side of the equation
- Initially focus on one element found on each side of the equation
- Balance one element at a time

The teacher reviews the steps with the whole class and then has students individually identify and focus on one of the steps and think about its place in the overall process. Each student identifies one step they consider to be critical and devises ways to make the step more efficient. Students then try out the process with their new step and discuss the results in terms of making the process more efficient.

Complexity across the grade levels for reasoned elaborations is a function of the extent to which students, as opposed to the teacher, control the steps of the procedure that are altered and the complexity of the procedure to which reasonable elaborations are applied. Other ways to manipulate the difficulty of reasoned elaboration tasks include

- having students make reasoned elaborations using complex procedures with embedded subprocedures; and
- when students' hypotheses are incorrect, having them explain the errors in their thinking.

Using the Habits of Mind

Two dispositions that are particularly applicable when first learning procedural knowledge are seeking clarity and taking incremental steps.

Seeking Clarity

The disposition of seeking clarity involves students being aware of when they are unsure about specific information and then rectifying the situation. A process for seeking clarity the teacher might present to students includes the following:

- Identify if something is unclear to you.
- Identify a question you need to ask to become more clear.
- Ask your question and seek the answer.

One of the best ways to introduce the habit of mind of seeking clarity is when students are first learning the various components of a step-by-step process. As the teacher describes a step-by-step process she has created, she can occasionally stop and ask students to identify what they are unclear about. Next, the teacher would explain to students that the more precise they can be regarding what they are unclear about, the better they will be able to formulate a question. As students articulate their questions, the teacher discusses with them the thinking they engaged in to arrive at their questions. Finally, the teacher provides time for students to work in small groups to answer each other's questions. As students become more independent with the process for seeking clarity, the teacher has them periodically evaluate themselves.

A self-assessment scale students might use with this disposition includes the following:

4. I've been seeking clarity without any teacher reminders.

3. I've been aware of when I'm not seeking clarity, but I still don't do a good job of identifying questions and seeking answers.

2. I've been trying to seek clarity when the teacher reminds me, but not otherwise.

1. I really haven't been trying to seek clarity.

Taking Incremental Steps

Taking incremental steps is a critical disposition when learning complex procedures with embedded subprocedures because it helps students avoid becoming overwhelmed by myriad interacting parts. A process for this disposition a teacher might present to students includes the following:

▶ Ask yourself: *What is one small part of this process I should work on?*

▶ Work on this small part until you feel comfortable and then move on to other small parts.

Complex procedures, by definition, have many interacting subprocedures. When a teacher is presenting a complex procedure like building a website using JavaScript, the teacher would first make students aware of all the steps involved. However, once students have an overview of the process, the teacher would focus their attention on smaller segments that still contain a significant number of steps. The teacher would encourage students to subdivide these steps into even smaller segments and learn these smaller steps to a point where they feel comfortable with them. The teacher would then encourage students to move to another small segment and continue the incremental approach until they have addressed all the steps within the complex procedure. As students utilize this disposition, the teacher would periodically have them evaluate themselves using the following scale:

4. I've been taking small steps without any teacher reminders.

3. I've been aware of when I should be taking small steps, but I still don't do a good job of trying to do so.

2. I've been trying to take small steps when the teacher reminds me, but not otherwise.

1. I really haven't been trying to take small steps.

Cognitive Analysis Questions

The cognitive analysis processes addressed in this chapter are analyzing errors for procedures and reasoned elaborations with procedures.

Questions that might be used with tasks that involve analyzing errors for procedures include:

▸ What are some of the characteristics of the errors (i.e., bugs) you found in this procedure you were not aware of?

▸ What are some characteristics of the procedure you were not aware of?

▸ What was the most difficult part of identifying errors? Why?

Questions that might be used with tasks that involve making reasoned elaborations about procedures include:

▸ What are some characteristics you found in your reasoned elaborations about the procedure you were not aware of?

▸ What are some characteristics of this procedure you were not aware of?

▸ What was the most difficult part of analyzing your reasoned inferences about this procedure? Why?

Habits of Mind Questions

The two habits of mind that fit particularly well when learning procedural knowledge are seeking clarity and taking incremental steps.

Questions that might be used with seeking clarity include:

▸ What things do you become aware of that let you know you should be seeking clarity about a procedure?

▸ When you realize you aren't clear about a procedure, what emotions do you feel and what do you say to yourself?

▸ What's one small thing you can do to get better at seeking clarity about this procedure?

Questions that might be used with taking incremental steps include:

- What things do you become aware of that let you know you should be seeking incremental steps?

- When you realize you are not taking incremental steps, what emotions do you have and what do you say to yourself?

- What's one small thing you could do to get better at taking incremental steps?

Summary

This chapter addressed enhancing rigor when students are initially learning procedural knowledge. Critical to enhancing rigor in this situation is for the teacher to proceduralize content by creating step-by-step processes that become the focus of initial instruction. Teachers should also create worked examples based on these step-by-step processes. With these in place, the teacher can create rigor-enhancing tasks that involve the cognitive analysis process of analyzing procedures for the presence of errors or bugs. The teacher can also design tasks using the cognitive analysis process of making reasoned (if/then) elaborations. The habits of mind that are particularly useful when students are initially learning procedural knowledge include seeking clarity and taking incremental steps.

CHAPTER 5

Teaching the Cognitive Analysis Processes

Thus far we have addressed activities teachers can design that enhance the rigor with which students are approaching declarative and procedural knowledge. Recall from the introductory chapter that one component of rigor is discerning new relationships between topics and new distinctions within topics. The cognitive analysis processes as described in chapters 1 through 4 are designed to accomplish such purposes with declarative and procedural knowledge. In this chapter we focus on the cognitive analysis processes as a type of procedural knowledge in themselves which can and should be directly taught to students.

This perspective that cognitive analysis processes should be directly taught became popular in the United States during the "thinking skills" movement of the 1980s described in the introductory chapter (see Marzano et al., 1988). By definition, teaching the cognitive analysis skills involves presenting them to students as step-by-step processes and allowing students to practice these processes using content with which they are familiar.

It is important to note that the step-by-step processes described in this chapter are meant to be presented to and practiced by students. The processes described in chapters 1 through 4 are meant to be used by teachers to design tasks that will enhance rigor for students. As already noted, the cognitive analysis processes are themselves procedural knowledge and should be taught as such.

Teaching Comparing

Comparing is the cognitive analysis process of identifying and describing how two items are similar and/or different relative to specific characteristics. The steps in the cognitive analysis process of comparing can be described to students as follows:

1. Identify the items you wish to compare.
2. Identify the characteristics on which you wish to compare the items.
3. Identify how the items are similar and/or different on the characteristics.
4. Describe what you now know about the items that you didn't know before.

An important part of the comparing process, in terms of the extent to which it enhances rigor, is identifying the characteristics that will form the basis of the comparison. If characteristics are trivial, then little rigor will be produced. To illustrate, consider the task of comparing a democracy and a republic. If they are compared on the number of letters they contain, knowledge about the items is not enhanced. If they are compared on their recent histories, knowledge about them can be significantly enhanced.

Another important part of the comparing process a teacher might want to emphasize is that metaphors and similes are abstract types of comparing. To illustrate, consider the metaphor *love is a rose*. On the surface they have few if any characteristics in common. However, if one considers the following abstract characteristics, then these two seemingly unrelated topics can be compared:

- How alluring they are
- How they can be dangerous

A simpler version of the comparing process that can be stated in the form of questions is:

- What do I want to compare?
- What do I want to compare them on?
- How are they similar and/or different?

When teaching cognitive analysis processes, students should have a chance to practice the processes with content they know quite well. This puts the focus on learning the cognitive analysis process and not on new content because students are already familiar with that content. Practice activities a teacher might use with students include:

- Have students compare two of the pets they have had.
- Have students compare two sports teams they know about.

Teaching Classifying

Classifying is the cognitive analysis process of identifying the category to which an item belongs based on specific characteristics or grouping items into categories based on specific characteristics. As described in previous chapters, there are two types of classification tasks. One type of classifying, identifying the category to which an item belongs, is referred to as superordinate classifying. The other type, grouping items into categories, is referred to as subordinate classifying.

Superordinate Classifying

The process for superordinate classifying might be initially presented to students in the following way:

1. Identify a specific item.
2. Describe the important characteristics of this item.
3. By examining the characteristics you have listed, determine if the item can be considered part of a bigger category.
4. Identify and list some of the characteristics of the bigger category.
5. Determine what the characteristics of the bigger category tell you about the item you started with.

The working dynamic of this process is that once you know the superordinate category to which an item belongs, you know more about the original item. For example, once you know that a dolphin is a type of mammal, you know more about dolphins. There is a flow of information from the superordinate category on down.

A simpler version of the superordinate classifying process might be described in the following way:

▶ What do I want to classify?
▶ What category does in fit into?
▶ What are some other things in the same category?
▶ Do these other things tell me something about my original item?

Practice activities that might be used include the following:

▶ Have students identify the superordinate category into which their favorite food belongs.
▶ Have students identify the superordinate category into which their favorite movie belongs.

Subordinate Classifying

The process for subordinate classifying might be presented to students in the following way:

1. Identify a specific category of items.
2. Identify and describe the items within the category.
3. Sort the items in the category into subcategories.
4. Describe what is unique about each subcategory and what is common to all subcategories.

The flow of information in this process is from the subordinate categories on up. The act of identifying subcategories provides new insights about the items that are classified. If you know that you want to buy a golden retriever, but then start studying the various types of golden retrievers, you will likely be much more knowledgeable about the golden retriever you wish to buy.

The following is a simpler version of the steps in this process that might be presented to students:

- Pick a group of things.
- What are some smaller groups within this bigger group?
- How are the smaller groups different?
- How are they all the same?
- What does this tell you about the overall group?

Practice activities in which you might engage students include:

- Have students list their friends and then organize them into subcategories.
- Have students list the songs they like and then organize them into subcategories.

Teaching Supporting Claims

Supporting claims is the process of building a hierarchic system of support for statements you believe to be true. The process of supporting claims can be presented to students in the following steps:

1. Identify whether you are stating an opinion that needs to be supported.
2. If so, state your opinion (i.e., claim) as clearly as possible.
3. To support your claim, provide one or more reasons (grounds) why you believe it to be true.
4. For each reason provide evidence (backing) that indicates your reasons are accurate.
5. If necessary, describe the circumstances (qualifiers) under which you believe your claim would not be valid.

When first teaching this process, a teacher might make the point that people make claims frequently and systematically. Anytime anyone is asserting that something is true, he or she is making a claim. The vast majority of the time, support is not needed because those claims occur in the context of informal discussions in which there are not expectations that people support what they say. However, if you are in a more formal discussion and trying to convince somebody that your claim is accurate, then you should adhere to the process for constructing support.

An important aspect of the constructing support process is articulating evidence (backing) for reasons (grounds). Where most people will provide reasons for what they believe is true, few will provide evidence to back up their reasons. Stated differently, most people state claims and provide grounds, but rarely provide backing for their grounds. Another part of the process to emphasize with students is describing the circumstances under which a claim is not true. The teacher should explain to students that this is called a qualifier, and that it's a way of clearly defining the limits of your support.

The following is a simpler version of this process that might be presented to younger students:

- What is a new idea I have that I want to communicate?
- What are my reasons for thinking this idea is true?
- What is the evidence for each reason?
- What are the situations for which my new idea might not be true?

Some practice activities that might be used with students include:

- Have students construct support for one of the two following claims: 1) We should have homework. 2) We should not have homework.
- Have students state and provide support about their favorite out-of-school activity.

Teaching Elaborating

Recall from the discussion in previous chapters that elaboration is a type of inference, and that there are two forms of elaboration: default elaborations and reasoned elaborations.

Default Elaborations

Default elaborations involve characteristics we assume are associated with information we are currently dealing with. Human beings engage in default elaborations quite naturally without even being aware of it. Making the elaboration process overt and conscious can provide students with insights into how their mind works. That process is relatively simple:

1. Identify the specific topic you are studying.
2. Identify those characteristics you believe are usually associated with that topic.
3. For each characteristic you have identified, check to make sure that it is consistent with what you are learning about the topic.
4. If there are inconsistences, try to determine what is accurate.

One important part of this process to emphasize with students is that they are continually engaged in making assumptions about people, places, things, and events. These assumptions come from our prior knowledge—what we have learned in the past. Many times our assumptions are accurate, but our assumptions can also be inaccurate. If we hear, read, or see anything that contradicts our assumptions, we should try to find out what is accurate. The following is a simpler version of this process that might be presented to students:

▶ What do I know about this person, place, thing, or event?

▶ Am I receiving new information that contradicts what I already know?

▶ If yes, how do I find out what's accurate: what I thought I knew or what I am learning now?

Some practice activities students might be involved in include:

▶ Have students examine their default elaborations about their friends.

▶ Have students examine their default elaborations about movie stars or famous singers.

Reasoned Elaborations

Reasoned elaborations are not based on assumptions we have stored in permanent memory. Rather, these types of inferences are created newly as we are interacting with content. We come up with an idea that seems reasonable and we try it out. These types of elaborations work best with procedural knowledge because we can test our predictions and see the results. The following is a process that can be presented to students:

1. Given what you know so far about this process, what are some predictions you can make about what would happen if you changed something.

2. Think of a change to make in the process that would make it more effective.

3. Try making the change with your prediction in mind.

4. Examine what happens to see if it confirmed your prediction.

5. If not, reexamine your thinking and make another change.

An important aspect of this process to reinforce with students is that it represents the way human beings learn and adapt procedural knowledge. Once we learn a procedure, like how to hit a golf ball with a specific club like a driver, we can run into situations where the process we originally learned doesn't work very well. For example, the process we learned using a driver might work well when hitting from a tee, but doesn't work well when hitting a golf ball that is lying in rather tall grass. In such cases, we have to make adaptations using the skill of reasoned inference.

The following is a simpler process that might be presented to students:

- How do I usually go about this process?
- What steps do I use?
- How will I change the process to make it better?
- How well did it work?

Practice activities to use with students might include:

- Ask students to change a routine they currently use at home to make it more efficient, like getting ready for school.
- Ask students to change a routine they use at school to make it more effective.

Teaching Analyzing Errors

Error analysis is the process of identifying errors in information you are learning or procedures you are learning. As this definition indicates, there are two approaches to analyzing errors—one for declarative knowledge and one for procedural knowledge.

Analyzing Errors with Declarative Knowledge

Analyzing errors with declarative knowledge involves determining if the new information you are experiencing about a topic contains common errors in reasoning. One of the first things to do when teaching this cognitive analysis skill is to provide students with a grounding in the common types of errors made with information. As described in previous chapters, there are four general categories of common errors in reasoning each with its own unique types of errors. There are described in Table 5.1:

Table 5.1. *Common errors in reasoning*

Faulty Logic
a. **Contradiction.** Presenting conflicting information to support a claim. For example, if a senator says she is for a tax increase and then later says she is against a tax increase, she has committed the *fallacy* of contradiction.
b. **Accident.** Failing to recognize that your evidence is based on an exception to a rule. For example, concluding that the letter *e* always comes before the letter *i* after observing the spelling of the words *neighbor* and *weigh* is an example of an accident.

(Continued)

Table 5.1.   *Common errors in reasoning* (continued)

Faulty Logic

c. ***False cause.*** *False cause* occurs when someone confuses a temporal (time) order of events with causality or when someone oversimplifies a very complex causal network. For example, if someone concludes that the decision to place a man on the moon was directly caused by America's failed attempt to send a satellite into orbit, he is confusing temporal order with causality. False cause also occurs when you oversimplify a cause. For example, if a person describes only one or two causes of the Civil War, he is making the error of false cause because the reasons for the Civil War were numerous and complexly related.

d. ***Begging the question (circularity).*** Making a claim and then supporting it with similar statements that do not constitute evidence. For example, if you say, "That product is not very useful," and then back up your assertion by saying, "You can't do anything with it," you are backing up one statement with another that means just about the same thing

e. ***Evading the issue.*** Sidestepping an issue by changing the topic. For example, if when asked about his involvement in arms trading to foreign countries, someone changes the topic of conversation to the necessity of weapons, he is evading the issue.

f. ***Arguing from ignorance.*** Supporting a claim simply because its opposite cannot be proven. For example, arguing that there is no intelligent life beyond the planet Earth because we cannot prove that life exists elsewhere is arguing from ignorance.

g. ***Composition and division.*** Asserting that something is true about the whole because it is true about one of the parts (composition), or asserting that something is true about a part because it is associated with the whole (division). For example, you are making an error of composition if you assume that all members of a family are intelligent because a single member of the family is. On the other hand, you are making an error of division if you conclude that a specific city in the state of Oregon receives a lot of rain simply because the state as a whole is noted for its rainfall.

Attacks

h. ***Poisoning of the well.*** Attacking everything that is offered in opposition to your own position. This type of attack manifests as a person being unwilling to listen to or consider anything contradictory to her opinion.

i. ***Arguing against the person.*** Making derogatory comments about anyone who is arguing against your position. For example, if a politician rejects another politician's stance on nuclear disarmament by attacking the person's heritage, he is arguing against the person.

j. ***Appealing to force.*** Threatening to psychologically or physically harm anyone who is arguing against your position. Telling someone that you will not like her anymore unless she takes your side on an issue is an example of appealing to force.

Table 5.1.   *Common errors in reasoning* (continued)

Weak Reference

k. ***Using sources that reflect habitual and confirmatory biases.*** Referencing sources that contain habitual bias or confirmatory bias. Habitual biases sometimes are unconsciously built into our thinking. For example, we might have a bias toward rejecting ideas from a specific radio talk show host or accepting ideas from a specific television network. Confirmatory bias involves only accepting information that supports what we believe and rejecting information that is contrary to our position.

l. ***Using sources that lack credibility.*** Using sources that have no documented record of being knowledgeable about a topic or who are known for providing inaccurate information. Information relevant to a topic or issue might come from sources that lack credibility. For example, only using information from an article that lacks citations would be an example of using a source that lacks credibility.

m. ***Appealing to authority.*** Relying on one's superior status (e.g., socially, corporately) as the evidence that your claim is true. For example, someone is appealing to authority if he says something is true (or false) simply because it is stated by a superior.

n. ***Appealing to the people.*** Asserting that your claim is true because it is a popular position. For example, supporting the claim that "staying up late does not affect my schoolwork" by stating that everyone in school stays up late is an example of appealing to the people.

o. ***Appealing to emotion.*** Eliciting emotion in support of your claim as the primary evidence that it is true. For example, when a speaker tries to convince people to vote for a particular political candidate by relating a story about the death of the candidate's family in a tragic accident, he is appealing to emotion.

Misinformation

p. ***Confusing the facts.*** Distorting or modifying facts to support your claim. For example, inaccurately describing a particular sequence of events as evidence for your claim would be an example of confusing the facts.

q. ***Misapplying a concept or generalization.*** Using inaccurate information about a concept or generalization to support your claim. For example, If someone claims that protesters at a rally at city hall should be arrested because they are committing "treason," they are misapplying the concept of treason.

Note: Adapted from Marzano and Pickering (1997).

Table 5.2. *Exercises for faulty logic*

In this exercise you are asked to identify errors referred to as "faulty logic." There are seven types of faulty logic errors:

- Contradiction
- Accident
- False cause
- Begging the question
- Evading the issue
- Arguing from ignorance
- Composition and division

For each example that follows, identify the type of faulty logic illustrated and be prepared to explain your answer.

1. Following the corporate scandal at Enron, the US economy experienced an economic slump and Mary was laid off from her job. Mary says Enron caused her to lose her job.

   This is an example of: _____

2. Joe argues that Santa is real because Santa exists.

   This is an example of: _____

3. After observing an ambulance with its siren blaring speed through a red light, William concludes it is okay to drive through red lights.

   This is an example of: _____

4. Susan tells her friends in the school cafeteria that she hates broccoli. That same evening at dinner, Susan thanks her mom for making broccoli because it's one of her favorite foods.

   This is an example of: _____

5. Miss Jones argues that there is no cure for cancer because scientists have not discovered one yet.

   This is an example of: _____

6. President Lincoln was assassinated as the American Civil War came to an end. Mark concludes that the Civil War's end caused President Lincoln's assassination.

   This is an example of: _____

7. Because Colorado has a Republican governor, Julie concludes that all residents of Colorado are Republican..

   This is an example of: _____

8. When Walter's teacher asks him where his book report is, Walter tells his teacher that he admires the sweater she is wearing.

   This is an example of: _____

(Continued)

Table 5.2. *Exercises for faulty logic* (continued)

9. Because water is wet, Rick concludes that the elements that make water (hydrogen and oxygen) must also be wet.

    This is an example of: _____

10. On her way to school, Ann drives 50 mph in a 40 mph zone because she's late for school.

    This is an example of: _____

As the various types of errors in reasoning are presented to students, discussed, and exemplified, the teacher should provide practice activities like those in Table 5.2.

With a grounding in the various types of errors in reasoning, students can more readily perform the steps involved in the process of analyzing errors with declarative knowledge:

1. Determine if the new information you are receiving is intended to persuade you and, if so, does it contain anything that is unusual or surprising to you or something that just doesn't seem to fit?

2. Analyze the information for the common types of errors you have studied.

3. If you find any such errors, reject that information as unreliable.

4. If not, tentatively consider the information as accurate.

One of the more important things to point out about this process is that you use it when someone is trying to persuade you about something. When that is the case, you should become more vigilant than you normally would be.

The following is a simpler version of the process that might be presented to students:

▶ Is this information designed to convince me of something?

▶ Are there some facts that don't seem accurate or true?

▶ What kind of errors can I find here?

Some practice activities a teacher might present to students include:

▶ Have students find advertisements on the Internet that contain one or more errors in reasoning.

▶ Have students look for some common errors in reasoning when they interact with others.

Analyzing Errors with Procedural Knowledge

The process of analyzing errors with procedural knowledge is used when you are first learning a procedure. To use this cognitive analysis process, you must have some idea of the steps involved in the procedure. Ideally, these have been presented to students as step-by-step processes or in some other way (e.g., a demonstration by the teacher, a video demonstration, a written description, a flowchart).

The process that might be presented to students involves the following steps:

1. Make sure you are clear about the steps you are supposed to use when executing this procedure.
2. Go over the steps in your mind and imagine what they require you to do.
3. Try out each step, taking time to ensure you are doing it correctly.
4. When you are done, determine any step or steps you think you did incorrectly or were unsure about and make changes to make them more effective.
5. Go over the steps one at a time in your head again and then retry the procedure.

One of the more important things to emphasize about this process is that there are many ways to execute a procedure. Although it's important to compare the way you execute a process with recommended methods, it's also legitimate and sometimes necessary to use adaptations that fit your specific needs or requirements.

The following is a simpler version of the process:

▶ What are the steps in this process I'm supposed to use?
▶ What are the steps I use?
▶ How are they similar and different?
▶ What should I change?

Some simple practice activities include:

▶ Have students find famous artists or athletes who use procedures that run contrary to what is typically done.
▶ Have students identify procedures they do differently than the way others do it.

Summary

Previous chapters have addressed cognitive analysis processes as frameworks teachers use to design tasks that enhance the rigor with which students interact with declarative and procedural knowledge. This chapter addressed teaching the cognitive analysis processes as skills students can use on their own. For each cognitive analysis process, a step-by-step process was provided that can be taught to students. It is important to remember that when teaching the cognitive analysis processes, students should practice them using content with which they are already familiar so that the emphasis is on learning the process as opposed to learning new academic content.

CHAPTER 6

Teaching the Habits of Mind

The habits of mind are the tools that allow students to discern new distinctions about themselves as learners. As mentioned in the introductory chapter, this is one aspect of rigor. Directly teaching the habits of mind as a regular part of the curriculum can be one of the more powerful forms of curriculum change in which a school can engage. In previous works, I have referred to this type of change as transformational in its potential (Marzano, 2018). This is because habits of mind are probably the most transferrable skills one can learn. Resisting impulsivity, for example, is not only useful in school, but it is also useful in making life decisions, whether they be mundane or life altering. The same is true for virtually all of the other habits of mind. The dispositions represent a curriculum for success in life, not just a curriculum for academic success.

Recall that, in this book, I have highlighted seven dispositions for habits of mind, which are depicted in Table 6.1.

Teaching habits of mind is a little more complex and abstract than teaching cognitive analysis skills because habits of mind are a blend of strategies and attitudes or beliefs, whereas cognitive analysis skills are limited to procedures. For each habit of mind, then, teachers must initially provide some steps, but they must also address some potentially long-held beliefs students might have. Additionally, as indicated in the third column of Table 6.1, habits of mind typically work against some natural human tendencies that may be deeply engrained in students' behaviors.

It's important to realize that each habit of mind takes a great deal of time to develop. This is the case with all habits. To effectively develop the daily habit of exercise one must start with short, simple exercise routines that might be sporadically executed and then progress to larger, more complex routines that are executed systematically and frequently. The same holds true for habits of mind. Throughout the K–12 curriculum, students should begin with simple versions of each habit of mind that they use when reminded by the teacher. Over time, students progress up to complex versions of each habit of mind that they use in their daily lives, both in and out of school. In this chapter we consider how to teach and reinforce each habit of mind.

Table 6.1. *Habits of mind*

Disposition	Description	Natural Tendency It Overcomes
Staying focused when answers and solutions are not apparent	Recognizing you have become frustrated because you can't find an answer or solution and continuing to try	Tending to give up when we can't find answers of solutions
Seeking accuracy	Recognizing when it's important to be accurate and seeking resources to confirm your accuracy	Believing that being accurate about what we conclude or say is inconsequential
Resisting impulsivity	Recognizing when you are making decisions or generating conclusions too quickly	Making decisions and generating conclusions without much thought
Seeking clarity	Recognizing when you do not understand important content and taking steps to clear up misunderstandings	Believing that we understand something well when we don't
Developing fluency	Recognizing when you must balance speed and accuracy when executing a procedure and taking steps to do so	Being able to execute a procedure with relative competency but not being willing to develop it to a high level of efficiency
Seeking cohesion and coherence	Recognizing when content is comprised of small units that interact to form a unified whole and attending to both	Focusing on specific pieces of a complex system but not paying attention to the whole
Taking incremental steps	Recognizing when a situation involves multiple steps that cannot be approached as a whole and breaking it into smaller parts	Taking on too much at once when learning a complex system

Staying Focused When Answers and Solutions Are Not Apparent

The habit of mind of staying focused when answers and solutions are not apparent works against the natural human tendency to give up when we can't find answers. This is not necessarily a bad tendency. If we didn't have a limit on how many times we are willing to keep trying solutions to the same problem, we'd waste a great deal of time. But it's probably safe to say that most people give up much too early in the process and, consequently, do not allow themselves enough time to think about why they are stuck and what they should do about it.

Table 6.2 describes the progression of expectations across the K–12 curriculum for staying focused when answers and solutions are not apparent.

At the primary level, the teacher helps students understand that giving up when answers and solutions are not apparent is a bad habit to develop. Teachers might introduce this idea to students and then provide examples from their own lives. Students would then be invited to provide examples of situations where they give up. Some students might note that they give up when they are asked to solve problems in certain classes. Others might describe situations outside of school where they tend to give up such as their involvement in a sports team. At this level, when asked by the teacher, students should also be able to recognize when they are persevering and when they are not.

At the upper elementary level, expectations are that students understand common mistakes people make when trying to solve difficult problems such as staying with a possible solution even though it's obvious that it's not working. Staying with a solution is important, but it's also important to recognize when it's time to try another solution. At this level, students can also execute a relatively simple procedure that has been provided by the teacher. The teacher should emphasize that the critical part of this procedure is identifying what is stopping them from finding a solution. If they can pinpoint what they are missing or what is confusing them, they have taken a big step in finding a solution.

At the middle school level, students have a clear understanding of the type of thinking that occurs when this habit of mind is executed. Perhaps the most important part of such understanding for students is becoming aware of their inner dialogue relative to a specific habit of mind. Even though we are usually not aware of it, we are constantly involved in an inner dialogue. Relative to a particular habit of mind, our inner dialogue is frequently supporting the natural human tendency that is the opposite of the habit of mind. For example, our inner dialogue relative to staying focused when answers and solutions are not apparent usually tells us to give up because we can't solve that particular problem.

Table 6.2. *Expectations for staying focused when answers and solutions are not apparent*

Grade Level Band	Description
High School (Grades 9–12)	**The student will:** • Articulate specific situations in which he or she should stay focused when answers or solutions are not immediately apparent, use a personalized strategy involving self-analysis in those situations, and analyze the extent to which the strategy is effective. • Articulate a personalized strategy involving self-analysis (created or adapted from previously learned strategies) for staying focused when answers or solutions are not immediately apparent, such as taking a break when frustrated and then reengaging, or defining self-talk phrases or reflection questions that aid in using this disposition.

Middle School (Grades 6–8)	**The student will:**
	• Recognize when he or she is not staying focused and be able to carry out a complex strategy that involves self-analysis that is provided by the teachers, such as:
	  ○ Ask yourself if you have stopped trying.
	  ○ If yes, see if you can identify what is stopping you from trying harder.
	  ○ Tell yourself that you are going to give it a few more tries.
	  ○ When you've stopped trying, ask yourself what you've learned from the experience.
	• Understand what an individual might think and say to themselves while staying focused when answers or solutions are not immediately apparent, such as thinking: *Let me try that again* or *Maybe there's a different way to do this*.

Upper Elementary (Grades 3–5)	**The student will:**
	• When cued by the teacher, be able to carry out a simple teacher-provided strategy for staying focused when answers or solutions are not immediately apparent, that includes steps like the following:
	  ○ Ask yourself: *What am I trying to accomplish right now?*
	  ○ Try to describe what is frustrating you or what it is you can't find or solve.
	  ○ Tell yourself you are going to give it at least one more try and then do so.
	• Understand common mistakes or pitfalls associated with staying focused when answers or solutions are not immediately apparent, such as repeatedly using the same ineffective approach instead of trying a new solution.

Table 6.2. *Expectations for staying focused when answers and solutions are not apparent* (continued)

Grade Level Band	Description
Primary (Grades K–2)	**The student will:** • Accurately recognize when he or she is or is not staying focused when answers or solutions are not immediately apparent when provided with prompts by the teacher, like: "Are you giving up right now?" and "If you can't figure out the answer, do you notice yourself getting frustrated?" • Understand that giving up when answers or solutions are not immediately apparent is a bad habit to develop because it prevents us from solving difficult problems.

Our inner dialogue commonly generates emotions that are negative if our inner dialogue is negative. Fortunately, our inner dialogue can be changed. Becoming aware of and controlling what we say to ourselves and the emotions associated with that dialogue is one of the most powerful forms of metacognitive self-control. In Chapters 1 through 4, this was an explicit part of each of the habits of mind questions presented at the end of each chapter.

Additionally, at the middle school level, students can also execute a more sophisticated procedure without being cued by the teacher. This means they know when to use it without being reminded by the teachers. One important part of that procedure teachers should emphasize to students is identifying what is stopping them from trying harder. Another important part of the process is students summarizing what they have learned as a result of using the habit of mind.

At the high school level, the emphasis is on students' independence with this habit of mind. This begins with students developing their own strategy for persevering when answers and solutions are not immediately apparent. These strategies should demonstrate students' awareness of personal habits and beliefs that stop them from persevering. That is, the strategies students create should explicitly address the specific habits and beliefs that they must be aware of and control. Commonly, such habits and beliefs will include, for instance, thoughts or inner dialogue that they are simply not talented in a particular area and, therefore, trying hard won't pay off. At the high school level, students are actively employing their personal strategies outside of school and examining and reporting on the effectiveness of their strategies.

Seeking Accuracy

The habit of mind of seeking accuracy works against the natural human tendency to believe that it is okay to be inaccurate about what is said or concluded. In our day-to-day lives, this human tendency works quite well because most of the information we deal with has little impact on our lives or the lives of others. If the information we hear on the news about next week's predicted weather is not very accurate, it matters little to our lives. If we aren't accurate when we recount what we did on our vacation last year, it affects our life and that of others very little. But there are situations for which accuracy, or lack thereof, can have consequences. This habit of mind involves discerning which situations require a high degree of accuracy and having strategies to obtain accuracy when the situation warrants it.

There is an important distinction to make among the cognitive skills of analyzing errors for declarative knowledge, analyzing errors for procedural knowledge, and seeking accuracy. Analyzing errors for declarative knowledge involves critically examining information that we are receiving. Analyzing errors for procedural knowledge involves identifying and correcting errors or "bugs" in procedures. The habit of mind of seeking accuracy is not so much about finding errors as is it about ensuring that our statements and conclusions are as precise as is required by the immediate situation. It is also about discerning situations when accuracy is critical and when it is not.

Table 6.3 describes the progression of expectations across the K–12 continuum.

At the primary level, students should begin to recognize some indicators that they should be using this habit of mind. For example, students should recognize that when they hear or read something that strikes them as hard to believe, it is probably important to seek accuracy so that they might use this information accurately if they are to repeat it. Implicit in this awareness is the realization that not everything they hear, see, or read is necessarily accurate so they should not repeat it without seeking accuracy. In fact, with the advent of the Internet, it is quite easy for people to put out information that is either inaccurate or completely false. At the primary level, teachers provide students with situations where it might be useful to seek accuracy and then ask them if they are thinking about if the information is accurate. For example, the teacher might present video recordings of content from the Internet and ask students whether they think the information is something about which they might want to seek accuracy.

At the upper elementary level, students expand their understanding of seeking accuracy by recognizing common pitfalls or mistakes people make when using this disposition, such as relying on one source only. The teacher might engage students in activities demonstrating how only using a single source can result in false conclusions. At this level, students can also execute a

Table 6.3. *Expectations for seeking accuracy*

Grade Level Band	Description
High School (Grades 9–12)	**The student will:** • Articulate specific situations in which he or she should seek accuracy, use a personalized strategy involving self-analysis in those situations, and analyze the extent to which the strategy is effective. • Articulate a personalized strategy involving self-analysis (created or adapted from previously learned strategies) for seeking accuracy (e.g., creating a checklist of indicators that the information they are assuming is accurate might not be).

Middle School (Grades 6–8)	**The student will:**
	• Be able to recognize when he or she is not seeking accuracy and carry out a complex procedure that involves self-analysis with steps provided by the teacher, like:
	  ◦ Ask yourself if there is something about which you need to seek accuracy.
	  ◦ If yes, identify possible resources (you might need to ask for help on this).
	  ◦ Check the sources you've identified.
	  ◦ Identify what you were right about, what you were wrong about, and what you have learned that is new.
	• Understand what an individual might think and say to themselves while seeking accuracy (e.g., feeling skeptical; thinking: *Am I sure about the sources I am trusting? Could they be biased? How thorough is the evidence they are presenting?*).

Upper Elementary (Grades 3–5)	**The student will:**
	• When cued by the teacher, be able to carry out a simple teacher-provided strategy for seeking accuracy that includes steps like the following:
	  ◦ Identify something about which you want to seek accuracy.
	  ◦ Identify some source you might use.
	  ◦ Consult your source.
	• Recognize common mistakes or pitfalls associated with seeking accuracy (e.g., relying on only one source).

Primary (Grades K–2)	**The student will:** • Accurately recognize when he or she is or is not seeking accuracy when provided with prompts by the teacher (e.g., "Are you thinking about the accuracy of this new information?"). • Be able to explain that seeking accuracy is very important in our society (e.g., because it's easy to put false information on the Internet).

simple procedure for seeking accuracy that has been provided by the teacher. The teacher should emphasize that the important part of this procedure is finding an available source that you can trust as being accurate. Usually there is a trade-off that has to be made between availability of a source and how sure you are about its accuracy. That is, many times, sources that are readily available might not be the most accurate.

At the middle school level, students should have a mental model of what they should be saying to themselves if they are using this habit of mind. Again, an important part of this model is controlling their inner dialogue. When executing this disposition, that dialogue should include a great many questions about the content they are learning. They can also recognize when they should be seeking accuracy but are not, and carry out a relatively complex procedure provided by the teacher that involves self-analysis. A critical aspect of the procedure at this level is identifying what they were initially right about and what they were initially wrong about prior to seeking accuracy.

At the high school level, students create their own strategies for seeking accuracy. Again, these strategies explicitly address their personal habits and beliefs that work against them when seeking accuracy in school and outside of school. Teachers might encourage students to share these strategies and build a class list of the resources associated with seeking accuracy. Students can also report on how they use this disposition outside of school and the results they have noticed.

Resisting Impulsivity

The habit of mind of resisting impulsivity is intended to mitigate the human tendency to make decisions and generate conclusions quickly and without much thought. A case can be made that impulsivity is rarely very useful except in situations where we are engaging in behaviors that are routine and don't require much conscious thought. For example, what we do in the morning after we wake up is certainly routine and doesn't require much thought on our part. So, it makes little sense to refer to such behavior as impulsive. It is also true that sometimes we have to make quick decisions in times of crisis. But such actions are not necessarily impulsive. If we have developed useful rules for our behavior, making a quick decision in an emergency is certainly legitimate.

Table 6.4 describes the progression of expectations across the K–12 curriculum.

At the primary level, students should understand some of the benefits of resisting impulsivity, such as you tend not to make mistakes that you have to go back and fix later. As an example, teachers might provide students with a passage and ask them to read it as quickly as they can and then ask them what

Table 6.4. *Expectations for resisting impulsivity*

Grade Level Band	Description
High School (Grades 9–12)	**The student will:** • Articulate specific situations in which he or she should resist impulsivity, use a personalized strategy involving self-analysis in those situations, and analyze the extent to which the strategy is effective. • Articulate a personalized strategy involving self-analysis (created or adapted from previously learned strategies) for resisting impulsivity (e.g., defining certain emotions as cues to consider conclusions and decisions more carefully, reflecting on the differences between the likely outcomes of the original impulsive decision and the outcomes of the reasoned decision).

Middle School (Grades 6–8)	**The student will:**
	• Recognize when he or she is not resisting impulsivity and respond by executing a complex teacher-provided strategy involving self-analysis with steps like the following:
	  ○ Ask yourself if this is a situation where you should stop and think before you form a conclusion or do something.
	  ○ If yes, identify the conclusion you've already formed or the action you are about to take.
	  ○ Try to determine if you could form a better conclusion or take a better course of action and, if yes, do so.
	  ○ Identify what you've learned about the situation.
	• Understand what an individual might think and say to themselves while resisting impulsivity (e.g., feeling emotional at first; thinking: *Wait, let me stop and think about this more carefully*).

Upper Elementary (Grades 3–5)	**The student will:**
	• When cued by the teacher, be able to carry out a simple teacher-provided strategy with steps like the following:
	  ○ Stop for a moment and think about you're about to do.
	  ○ Ask yourself: *Is there anything about what I'm thinking of doing that I think I should change?*
	  ○ Once you've thought about your reaction, go ahead and act.
	• Recognize common mistakes or pitfalls associated with resisting impulsivity (e.g., delaying a decision but failing to actually consider other perspectives or new information).

(Continued)

Table 6.4.   *Expectations for resisting impulsivity* (continued)

Grade Level Band	Description
Primary (Grades K–2)	**The student will:** • Accurately recognize when he or she is or is not resisting impulsivity when provided with prompts by the teacher, such as: "Are you reacting impulsively right now when you should be stopping to think about things?" • Understand that resisting impulsivity is very important to being an effective learner because you tend not to make as many mistakes that you have to go back and fix later.

they remember about the passage, noting how rushing through something you're trying to learn doesn't produce very good results. One of the more important things to point out about this disposition is that impulsivity when making important decisions can have very negative consequences. The teacher might provide examples of this from his or her own life. As students are involved in challenging tasks, the teacher might have them stop and determine if they need to be thinking more carefully about what they are doing.

At the upper elementary level, students understand that there are some potential pitfalls of resisting impulsivity, such as waiting so long that you don't act on a decision or conclusion or missing out on an opportunity because you don't act quickly enough. Students can also execute a simple strategy provided by the teacher. The critical part of this teacher-provided process is thinking about the possible consequence of what you are about to do. This simple action is the driving force behind resisting impulsivity.

At the middle school level, students have developed a mental model for what they say to themselves when they are resisting impulsivity. Their inner dialogue should involve asking themselves if what they are about to do is something that they should stop and think about. They also can execute a complex procedure provided by the teacher that involves self-analysis. A critical part of that procedure involves identifying conclusions that they might have already formed and determining if their conclusions should be reexamined.

At the high school level, students create their own strategies. An important and interesting part of these strategies should be the situations students identify as times when they tend to be particularly impulsive. Anecdotes about those times can be shared and discussed in class. As students try out their personal strategies outside of school, they can identify and describe the changes that have occurred in their lives and their interactions with other people.

Seeking Clarity

The disposition of seeking clarity works against the natural human tendency to conclude that we understand something well enough even when we don't. Most of the time, this perspective is harmless. For most of the information we encounter, it is not important that we have a clear understanding of it. For example, it is not important to be clear about what occurred in a popular movie or show. However, in academic situations like school, if we are not clear about content and don't stop to seek clarity, we might be impeded in our learning at later dates. If a student is unclear about converting fractions, she will have trouble later on when the types of fractions become more complex.

Table 6.5 describes the progression of expectations across the K–12 curriculum.

At the primary level, the teacher points out situations in which seeking clarity would be helpful to students. Students might be asked to identify those classes in which they get confused but are reluctant to ask clarifying questions. The teacher might describe some of the benefits of seeking clarity using anecdotes about times when she sought clarity and it paid off. Students would be invited to relate their own examples. At this level, students are able to identify if they are or are not seeking accuracy when cued by the teacher. This is best done when students are being exposed to new information that is fairly complex. The teacher should occasionally stop and ask students to monitor how well they are seeking clarity.

At the upper elementary level, students are exposed to the common pitfalls of seeking clarity such as realizing you are not clear about some important information but not taking the appropriate steps to become clear. The teacher should emphasize that clarity doesn't come all at once. We must keep asking clarifying questions. The teacher might describe situations in which clarity about something came to him in layers as he kept employing this habit of mind. If students can formulate questions that will help them understand things better, they have already increased their understanding. Hence, asking clarifying questions is the focus of the strategy presented to students at this level.

At the middle school level, students develop a model of the inner dialogue that occurs when a person is executing this disposition. The teacher might relate the type of inner dialogue she engages in when seeking clarity. The awareness to instill in students is that dialogue that helps foster this habit of mind includes saying to yourself that it's okay to be confused and to acknowledge that you are confused. The strategy students are expected to employ at this level is again presented and cued by the teacher, but it is relatively complex in that it involves students' self-analysis. At this level, when students ask a clarifying question, they then take steps to get that question answered. The teacher might have students use this process while they are watching a video recording involving

Table 6.5. *Expectations for seeking clarity*

Grade Level Band	Description
High School (Grades 9–12)	**The student will:** • Articulate specific situations in which he or she should seek clarity, use a personalized strategy involving self-analysis in those situations, and analyze the extent to which the strategy is effective. • Articulate a personalized strategy involving self-analysis (created or adapted from previously learned strategies) for seeking clarity (e.g., making a habit of going back through notes from earlier lessons and adding to, clarifying, or correcting information).

Middle School (Grades 6–8)	**The student will:**
	• Recognize when he or she is not seeking clarity and respond by executing a teacher-provided complex strategy involving self-analysis with steps like the following:
	  ○ Ask yourself if there is something about which you are unclear.
	  ○ If yes, identify the question or questions you would need answered to have a better understanding.
	  ○ Determine whether you will try to answer the question(s) yourself by seeking more information or who you will ask to answer your question(s).
	  ○ Get your question(s) answered.
	  ○ Identify what you were right about, what you were wrong about, and what you have learned that is new.
	• Understand what an individual might think and say to themselves while seeking clarity (e.g., thinking: *I'm not sure I understand this* or *What resources are available to help me clarify this?*).

Upper Elementary (Grades 3–5)	**The student will:**
	• When cued by the teacher, be able to carry out a simple teacher-provided strategy for seeking clarity that includes steps like the following:
	  ○ Identify something about which you are unclear.
	  ○ Identify the question(s) you would need to ask to become more clear.
	  ○ Ask your question(s).
	• Recognize common mistakes or pitfalls associated with seeking clarity (e.g., failing to revise knowledge after the initial learning process).

Table 6.5. *Expectations for seeking clarity* (continued)

Grade Level Band	Description
Primary (Grades K–2)	**The student will:** • Accurately recognize when he or she is or is not seeking clarity when presented with prompts by the teacher such as: "Are you thinking about whether you are clear or not about this information?" • Understand that seeking clarity is very important to being an effective learner (e.g., because otherwise you might learn incomplete or inaccurate information).

new information and then provide students with time to find answers to their clarifying questions.

At the high school level, students develop strategies for seeking accuracy that focus on specific situations where they are having trouble learning something. In many cases, simply recognizing that they are not clear about content and asking clarifying questions can have immediate and positive influences on their understanding. As students try this disposition in their lives outside of school, they can again relate anecdotes to share with their classmates.

Developing Fluency

The habit of mind of developing fluency works against the natural human tendency to execute a procedure with relative competence while not putting the necessary energy into developing the procedure to a level where it can be executed as quickly as possible with as few errors as possible. Maintaining fluency requires continued vigilance because it's easy for students to sink into a state of complacency regarding the execution of a complex procedure.

Table 6.6 describes the progression of expectations across the K–12 curriculum.

At the primary level, students should understand some of the benefits of seeking fluency, such as it makes you more efficient when using a procedure and helps ensure that you receive benefits from the procedure. The teacher can also point out that becoming fluent is hard work and they shouldn't get discouraged. The teacher might describe times when he developed fluency for a complex procedure. Periodically, the teacher should stop students while they are engaged in a specific complex procedure to see if students can accurately identify if they are thinking about their fluency.

At the upper elementary level, the teacher helps students understand that it's easy to forget to stay focused on both speed and accuracy when seeking fluency.

Table 6.6. *Expectations for developing fluency*

Grade Level Band	Description
High School (Grades 9–12)	**The student will:** • Articulate specific situations in which he or she should seek fluency, use a personalized strategy involving self-analysis in those situations, and analyze the extent to which the strategy is effective. • Articulate a personalized strategy involving self-analysis (created or adapted from previously learned strategies) for seeking fluency (e.g., selecting specific procedures that would benefit from more fluency, identifying specific parts of a complex procedure that need the most development, setting up a practice schedule to develop fluency with the selected procedures).

Middle School (Grades 6–8)	**The student will:**
	• Recognize when he or she is not seeking fluency and respond by executing a complex teacher-provided strategy involving self-analysis with steps like the following:
	  ○ Ask yourself if this is a time when you should be seeking fluency for this procedure.
	  ○ If yes, set a goal to monitor your speed and accuracy.
	  ○ Periodically ask yourself if you need to focus more on your speed or more on your accuracy.
	  ○ When you're done, ask yourself what you can do to continue improving your fluency.
	• Understand what an individual might think and say to themselves while seeking fluency (e.g., reminding yourself to keep switching your focus from speed to accuracy).

Upper Elementary (Grades 3–5)	**The student will:**
	• When cued by the teacher, be able to carry out a simple teacher-provided strategy with steps like the following:
	  ○ Before you start the process, focus your attention on trying to work as quickly as you can without making errors.
	  ○ As you work, occasionally stop and evaluate how quickly you are working and how accurately you are working.
	  ○ If you're not performing well in either one of these areas, focus your attention on that area for a while.
	  ○ When you're done, identify if there is something you can do to get better at your speed or your accuracy.
	• Recognize common mistakes or pitfalls associated with seeking fluency (e.g., focusing too much attention on speed and ignoring accuracy or focusing too much attention on accuracy and ignoring speed).

Table 6.6. *Expectations for developing fluency* (continued)

Grade Level Band	Description
Primary (Grades K–2)	**The student will:** • Accurately recognize when he or she is or is not seeking fluency when provided with prompts by the teacher like: "Are you seeking fluency right now or do you need to pay more attention to your speed or accuracy?" • Understand that seeking fluency is important because it helps ensure you are receiving the benefits of a specific procedure and using that procedure efficiently.

It's a balancing act in which they always have to keep both goals in mind. The process provided by the teacher at this level emphasizes the need for balance between these two important but somewhat competing dynamics. The teacher must set up specific situations to provide practice in this procedure. For example, while reading a passage at their grade level, students might be asked to read relatively quickly while maintaining an awareness of how well they are comprehending the information.

Again, at the middle school level, the nature and importance of inner dialogue when cultivating fluency is introduced and exemplified by the teacher. This disposition might be one that creates the most angst for students because it requires so much mental attention. It's very helpful if the teacher can relate personal stories about how difficult it can be to develop fluency for a complex procedure. As with all habits of mind at this level, a procedure for seeking fluency is provided by the teacher, but the expectation is that students will recognize when the procedure should be used and do so.

At the high school level, students create their own strategies for seeking fluency and develop a good understanding of the procedures in their lives where this disposition will be the most useful. It is probably the case that many complex procedures students identify are used outside of school. This is not only acceptable but highly desirable because it reinforces the awareness that habits of mind are tools to be used over one's entire life and that will benefit many aspects of our day-to-day lives.

Seeking Cohesion and Coherence

The habit of mind of seeking cohesion and coherence works against the natural human tendency to focus on specific pieces of a complex system while not paying enough attention to the larger picture. The most obvious example of this tendency occurs during writing. We might create a composition that has well-structured sections, but those sections may not fit together as an integrated whole.

Table 6.7 describes the progression of expectations across the K–12 curriculum.

At the primary level, the teacher provides examples of situations where seeking cohesion and coherence is necessary. Any endeavor that has a number of parts that must work together will usually suffice. For example, cooking a meal has a number of separate events that must occur, and they all must be done in such a way that they come together. At this level, students should be able to recognize if they are seeking cohesion and coherence when asked by the teacher. While students are engaged in complex tasks like making a display depicting an ecosystem, the teacher might periodically ask them if they are making sure all the parts make sense together.

At the upper elementary level, students understand some of the pitfalls of this habit of mind such as waiting until a project is finished before examining how the all pieces work together. To create this awareness, the teacher might provide anecdotes of times in her life when she might have made this mistake. Alternatively, the teacher might provide this awareness by allowing students to work on a rather complex project and wait until the end to let them discover that all the pieces do not work together as a whole. The teacher-designed process at this level is simple but effective. While students are engaged in a complex project, the teacher asks them to stop and identify the specific piece on which they are currently working. The teacher then asks students to examine how well it fits with the rest of the pieces they have worked on.

At the middle school level, students understand the types of things they should be saying to themselves when using this habit of mind, such as: *Are there missing or extraneous pieces of this project?* The teacher might make students aware of effective inner dialogue by thinking aloud as they work on a complex project. The teacher might also exemplify some types of inner dialogue that work against this disposition such as: "This is so complex that I could never keep track of all the pieces and parts." A critical aspect of the process provided by the teacher at this level is the final check that all the pieces and parts of what has been created work together effectively and efficiently.

The personal strategies created by students at the high school level should include an awareness of the types of projects they engage in where seeking cohesion and coherence is necessary for success. There should be a good many such projects outside of the school environment, and students should be experiencing and recognizing success from the use of this habit of mind. Again, reporting their experience to their peers can help reinforce the importance of this disposition.

Table 6.7. *Expectations for seeking cohesion and coherence*

Grade Level Band	Description
High School (Grades 9–12)	**The student will:** • Articulate specific situations in which he or she should seek cohesion and coherence, use a personalized strategy involving self-analysis in those situations, and analyze the extent to which the strategy is effective. • Articulate a personalized strategy involving self-analysis (created or adapted from previously learned strategies) for seeking cohesion and coherence (e.g., planning all the pieces of large projects in advance, including opportunities to review for cohesion and coherence throughout a project's timeline).
Middle School (Grades 6–8)	**The student will:** • Recognize when he or she is not seeking cohesion and coherence and respond by executing a complex teacher-provided strategy that involves self-analysis with steps like the following: ○ Ask yourself if this is a situation in which you need to make sure all the pieces and parts work together. ○ If yes, then identify which piece you are working on right now. ○ Determine how well the piece fits with the ones you've already developed. ○ Make any necessary changes in the new or old pieces to make them all fit. ○ When you are done, check to make sure that your project has a clear focus at the end. ○ Evaluate how well you used this habit of mind and what effect it had on the outcome of the project. • Understand what an individual might think and say to themselves while seeking cohesion and coherence (e.g., thinking: *Are there any missing or extraneous parts?* or *Is this the overall effect I envisioned?*).
Upper Elementary (Grades 3–5)	• When cued by the teacher, be able to carry out a simple teacher-provided strategy for making sure all the pieces and parts fit together that include steps like the following: ○ Identify which piece of the project you are working on right now. ○ Determine if that piece makes sense with the other pieces in the project. ○ If not, identify what changes you have to make in the new piece or the other pieces to make them all fit. • Recognize common mistakes or pitfalls associated with seeking cohesion and coherence (e.g., waiting until the project is complete before checking for cohesion and coherence).

(Continued)

Table 6.7. *Expectations for seeking cohesion and coherence* (continued)

Grade Level Band	Description
Primary (Grades K–2)	**The student will:** • Accurately recognize when he or she is or is not making sure that all the parts are working together when provided with prompts by the teacher such as: "Are you checking to make sure that what you are working on right now fits in with the other pieces of your project?" • Understand that when you are making something with a lot of parts, all the parts have to work together (e.g., the parts of an engine, the sentences of a paragraph).

Taking Incremental Steps

The habit of mind of taking incremental steps works against the natural human tendency to take on too much when learning something new. It is best applied when learning a new procedure or solving a problem that has many parts.

Table 6.8 describes the progression of expectations across the K–12 curriculum.

At the primary level, the teacher helps students become aware of general situations for which this disposition might be useful. As mentioned, using incremental steps works best when learning a new complex procedure or solving a complex problem. The teacher might make reference to complex procedures students have learned in class such as complex addition or subtraction problems that involve a number of steps. The teacher might remind students how they learned the process in layers going from simple to more complex. The teacher might also help students acquire the basic understanding that breaking things into small steps makes very complex things manageable. Finally, the teacher would provide opportunities for students to recognize when they are and are not using this habit of mind. While students are working on a complex project, the teacher would stop and ask students to consider how well they are doing at taking small steps and not getting overwhelmed by the project as a whole.

At the upper elementary level, students explore some of the pitfalls associated with seeking incremental steps. One of the more common is to make the incremental pieces so small that you forget the overall process you are trying to execute or learn. At this level, students would execute a simple teacher-designed process that provides some experience at breaking a process into small components. The critical part of the process at this level is to reinforce the importance of thinking in terms of small steps.

Table 6.8. *Expectations for taking incremental steps*

Grade Level Band	Description
High School (Grades 9–12)	**The student will:** • Articulate specific situations in which he or she should break tasks into small steps, use a personalized strategy involving self-analysis in those situations, and analyze the extent to which the strategy is effective. • Articulate a personalized strategy involving self-analysis (created or adapted from previously learned strategies) for breaking tasks into small steps (e.g., defining which parts should be completed first for common types of projects).

Middle School (Grades 6–8)	**The student will:**
	• Recognize when he or she is not seeking incremental steps and respond by executing a teacher-provided, complex strategy involving self-analysis with steps like the following:
	  ○ Ask yourself if this is a situation in which it would be useful to work in small steps.
	  ○ If yes, then identify the first small step you should take.
	  ○ Based on what you have accomplished in your first small step, identify the next small step to take and try it out.
	  ○ Keep trying small steps until you are done.
	  ○ When you are done with the task, ask yourself how well it turned out and what you learned about yourself.
	• Understand what an individual might think and say to him- or herself while seeking incremental steps (e.g., feeling overwhelmed at first, thinking about what small step can be taken right now).

Upper Elementary (Grades 3–5)	**The student will:**
	• When cued by the teacher, be able to carry out a teacher-provided strategy for breaking a problem into small steps, like the following:
	  ○ Ask yourself: *What is one small thing I could do to help solve this problem?*
	  ○ Try out that step and then ask yourself what other small thing you could do to help solve the problem.
	• Recognize common mistakes or pitfalls associated with seeking incremental steps (e.g., creating too many steps, forgetting to examine each part's relationship to the whole).

(Continued)

Table 6.8. *Expectations for taking incremental steps* (continued)

Grade Level Band	Description
Primary (Grades K–2)	**The student will:** • Accurately recognize when he or she is or is not seeking incremental steps when provided prompts by the teacher, like: "Are you breaking this into smaller steps?" • Understand that complex problems are more easily solved if you break them up into small steps (e.g., because you are less likely to get overwhelmed by a few small tasks than by one big one).

At the middle school level, students begin examining the inner dialogue that supports this disposition and the inner dialogue that does not. Inner dialogue that affirms to students that complex problems can be solved if you break them down into small pieces supports this habit. Inner dialogue that focuses on being overwhelmed does not. The teacher might lead students in identifying things to say to themselves when they start to feel overwhelmed, such as: *I'll just make this part work and then go on to the next part.* The teacher-designed process at this level focuses on the iterative nature of this disposition. Students execute small steps until they finally accomplish what they wanted to.

At the high school level, students create their own processes for seeking incremental steps and apply it to situations of their own choosing. An important realization students should come to by high school is that many seemingly unsolvable problems and issues can be successfully addressed if they are willing to iteratively and tirelessly apply small steps.

Summary

This chapter focused on explicitly teaching the habits of mind as a curriculum that is useful in school and in life. The emphasis was on gradually developing students' competence throughout the K–12 curriculum with the awareness that effective use of these dispositions involves executing increasingly more sophisticated strategies as well as cultivating a growing awareness of personal habits and beliefs that work against the use of these dispositions. Ultimately, the purpose of teaching habits of mind is to provide students with metacognitive self-control that they might use in any situation.

CHAPTER 7

Seeking Rigor in Project-Based Learning Through Knowledge Application Tasks

Project-based learning has wide acceptance and many different variations. I take the perspective that, in some if not many situations, projects tend to devolve into students selecting topics of interest and reporting out on them. Although this is a useful endeavor, it does not necessarily result in enhanced rigor. In this chapter, I present a way of designing projects that emphasizes the enhancement of students' options and use structures that provide for clear pathways to rigor.

The basic approach to doing this involves designing projects around cognitively complex tasks that have a specific structure to them. One of the reasons for this is that there are definable types of cognitively complex tasks that require the application of knowledge and have discernable structures. They are also commonly used in academic and nonacademic situations. Those tasks are problem-solving, decision-making, experimental inquiry, investigation, invention, and systems analysis. Indeed, many of the "projects" in which we engage in our day-to-day lives are centered around these processes.

Certainly, the goal of project-based instruction is for students to design their own projects. However, because these cognitively complex tasks are rather challenging and have unique characteristics, it is best to introduce them to students one at a time.

Problem-Solving

Problem-solving is probably the most flexible knowledge application task that can be applied to project-based learning. I say this because it can be used in both academic as well as nonacademic situations. Therefore, having students develop projects that focus on academic problems teaches them a highly transferable skill. At its core, problem-solving can be described as the process of addressing and overcoming constraints and limiting conditions that are impeding the accomplishment of a goal.

To introduce the problem-solving process, the teacher might present an example of a famous problem that was solved. For example, the teacher might describe some of the problems the Apollo 13 crew had to solve in 1970 on their failed mission to the moon. One of the problems was that carbon monoxide on the lunar module was building up. There were no more air filters designed for the lunar module; however, there were filters available that were designed for use in the command module. Unfortunately, these filters had a square hose, whereas the opening for the filter in the lunar module was round. Therefore, the crew of Apollo 13 had to design an adapter that allowed the square hose to fit into the round hole of the lunar module. They did this using material that was available like tape, cardboard, and even a sock worn by of one of the astronauts.

After discussing a famous problem with students, the teacher would point out some of the defining characteristics of problems and the problem-solving process, such as:

▶ It involves a goal for which there are constraints or limiting conditions.

▶ To solve a problem, you have to consider alternatives.

▶ You keep trying out alternatives until you've overcome the constraints or limiting conditions.

Once students have discussed problem-solving at a general level, the teacher would present them with a detailed set of steps for problem-solving, such as the following:

1. Identify the goal you wish to accomplish.

2. Identify any obstacles or limiting conditions that are in the way of accomplishing the goal.

3. Analyze the obstacles or limiting conditions to determine how they are stopping you from accomplishing your goal.

4. Identify and describe at least two solutions that could possibly be used to overcome the obstacles and limiting conditions you have identified.

5. Try out the possible solution that seems the best and involves resources that are readily available.

6. After you have tried out your solution, analyze how well it has worked.

7. If your problem is still not solved, try another solution you have identified or generate a new possible solution.

8. If you can't solve the problem, identify a related goal that you can accomplish.

Next, the teacher would demonstrate and exemplify these steps using a concrete problem. For example, the teacher might explain that he was leaving for work and realized his car wouldn't start. The first step in the process is to identify the goal. In this case, it's obvious—getting to work on time. The second step is to identify the obstacles or limiting conditions, which is that his typical means of transportation was not available. The teacher would continue to exemplify the various steps he used to try to get to work. Once students understand the problem-solving process, the teacher guides them in the design of a project such as the following.

> A US history class has been studying the nature and structure of the United Nations. The teacher explains that poor nations believe that they do not have strong enough voices in the UN, but wealthy nations, who impact trade and commerce on a worldwide scope, believe that they are more influential in world affairs and should have the greater say in UN discussions. The teacher poses the question: "How might the structure of the UN be revised to address the concerns of the poorer nations and the wealthier nations?" The teacher also helps students articulate the fact that it is the structure of the UN that represents the limiting conditions. As their project, students complete the rest of the problem-solving process.

Another option for creating projects around problem-solving is to investigate how historical problems were solved, such as the air filter problem in Apollo 13. Students would be asked to describe the following:

- The original goal
- The obstacle or constraining conditions
- The solutions that were considered
- Why the final solution was selected
- Whether an alternative goal had been considered

Recall that, in this book, I define rigor as discerning new relationships between content and new distinctions about content that have not been directly taught. Problem-solving projects require students to generate and describe new relationships—namely, the solutions that are hypothesized to overcome specific obstacles and limiting conditions. Problem-solving also requires students to discern new distinctions—specifically, the distinction between an obstacle and a limiting condition.

Decision-Making

Decision-making is the knowledge application process of generating and applying criteria to select between alternatives that appear equal. Like problem-solving, it is a process that can be used in academic situations and in life outside of school. The decision-making process can be introduced by describing famous decisions that have been made, such as the now infamous decision by Decca Records in 1962 to not sign the Beatles. Decca's reasons included criteria like people weren't interested in quartets, bands that relied on guitars were losing popularity, and British bands would not be accepted in the United States. Of course, as history has demonstrated, this was not a wise financial decision for Decca.

The teacher would use this example to discuss some of the defining characteristics of decision-making:

- It involves selecting among competing alternatives.
- It involves identifying the criteria on which alternatives will be judged.
- To some extent, all problems involve decisions but not all decisions involve problems.

Once decision-making has been addressed in general terms, students should be provided with a detailed decision-making process:

1. State the decision you are trying to make and the alternatives you are considering.
2. Describe the criteria you are using to select among the alternatives.
3. Assign a score (e.g., from 1 to 3) to each criterion to indicate its importance.
4. For each alternative, assign a score (e.g., from 1 to 3) indicating how well it meets each criterion.
5. Multiply the importance score for each criterion by the score indicating how well each alternative meets the criterion.
6. For each alternative, add up the products of the criterion importance scores and the scores indicating the extent to which the alternative met the criterion. Identify the alternative that has the most points as your decision.
7. Reexamine your criteria and alternatives to make sure you have made the right decision.

To illustrate this process, a teacher might present students with the example of when she was making a decision about where to go on vacation. The alternatives she was considering were San Diego, Orlando, and Denver. The criteria she was considering were:

A. Warm
B. Costs less than $1,000
C. Not too far from home

For step #3 involving importance scores, the teacher assigned the following scores:

A. Warm = 3
B. Costs less than $1,000 = 2
C. Not too far from home = 1

For step #4 involving the extent to which each alternative satisfies the criterion, the teacher assigned the following scores:

	San Diego	Orlando	Denver
A. Warm (3)	3	3	1
B. Less than $1,000 (2)	2	1	2
C. Not too far from home (1)	3	1	3

For steps #5 and #6 involving the multiplication and summation of scores, the teacher performed the following computation:

	San Diego	Orlando	Denver
A. Warm (3)	$3 \times 3 = 9$	$3 \times 3 = 9$	$1 \times 3 = 3$
B. Less than $1,000 (2)	$2 \times 2 = 4$	$1 \times 2 = 2$	$2 \times 2 = 4$
C. Not too far from home (1)	$3 \times 1 = 3$	$1 \times 1 = 1$	$3 \times 1 = 3$
Totals	16	12	10

Given these calculations, the teacher acknowledged that San Diego was the best choice given the alternatives that were considered and the criteria that were used.

For step #7, the teacher considered if she wished to reexamine the criteria or alternatives, but decided that this decision to go to San Diego adequately represents what she valued.

Once students understand the decision-making process, the teacher guides them in the design of projects like the following:

A theater teacher is working with the class to design a set for a play the setting for which is the Old West or the late 1800s. The teacher presents students with sketches of three possible versions of a suitable set and asks them to make a decision among them. They are to list the criteria they are using to make their selection along with the scores from steps #3, #4, #5, and #6 of the process and justify why they assigned the scores they did.

Another option for creating projects around decision-making is to investigate how historical decisions were made such as the decision President Truman made to drop an atomic bomb on Japan on August 6, 1945. Students would be asked to collect information on the decision and come up with reasonable estimates of:

▸ the different alternatives that were being considered;

▸ criteria that were used; and

▸ the scores Truman and his team likely assigned in steps #3, #4, #5, and #6 of the process.

Within the decision-making process, students must forge new relationships by the very process of cross-referencing criteria with alternatives. It is the criteria they select that renders their decisions rigorous or not. An important new distinction for students is that all criteria are not created equal. They should consider some criteria as more important than other criteria and make this explicit in the decision-making process.

Experimental Inquiry

Experimental inquiry is the knowledge application process of generating a hypothesis about a physical or psychological phenomenon and then testing your hypothesis. To introduce the experimental inquiry process, the teacher might describe some famous experiments such as those designed by Henry A. Landsberger in the 1920s and 1930s at the Hawthorne Works outside of Chicago, Illinois. Landsberger initially examined the findings from studies conducted at Hawthorne to determine whether the level of light within a building affects the productivity of workers. While the results supported the hypothesis that more light increased productivity, they also supported the hypothesis that the workers seemed to increase their productivity when they realized they were being studied. He hypothesized that the workers knew they were being studied, which made them feel important and work harder. He began to set up experiments that gave workers the impression they were being studied, but didn't involve any actual intervention that was designed to help them, such as more light. These studies confirmed his hypothesis that simply thinking that they were involved in some type of study increased workers' productivity. This phenomenon became known as the "Hawthorne effect."

Using this example, the teacher would point out some of the defining features of experimental inquiry, such as:

▸ It is an attempt to explain cause-and-effect relationships.

▸ It involves generating hypotheses and then testing them.

▸ Sometimes hypotheses are formed after observing a phenomenon.

The teacher would then provide students with a set of steps, like the following:

1. Identify something you have observed or wish to observe that is of interest to you.
2. After making some careful observations, describe the theories or rules you think explain the relationships you have observed.
3. Make a prediction about something that will happen or would happen under certain conditions.
4. Set up an activity that will directly test your prediction and carry it out.
5. Discuss the results of your activity in light of your prediction.
6. If necessary, change your original explanation of what happened and make a new prediction.
7. Set up another activity that will directly test your prediction.

The teacher might exemplify the steps using a simple example like the time he bought a new refrigerator. After a few days, he noticed that when he put food on the top shelf, it would almost be frozen when he took it out to eat it. He reasoned that the food on the top shelf was too close to the cooling coils at the top of the refrigerator, so he hypothesized that if he moved the food down, it wouldn't be so cold. The teacher moved the food down one shelf and found that the food was a little less cold but still too cold. The teacher then moved the food down to the bottom shelf, where he found that it wasn't cold enough. He realized that there was a simple, direct relationship between how close food was to the top of the refrigerator and how cold it stayed, and so he figured out that the middle of the refrigerator was just about right. He also realized that his solution was a temporary one, and he got the refrigerator fixed so that it cooled more evenly.

Once students have an understanding of the experimental inquiry process, the teacher guides them in the design of projects like the following:

A health teacher has students keep a log of their exercise routine over a two-week period. Students are told to note the time of day, how long before and after a meal, the type of meal, and how effective the exercise seemed to be. At the end of the two weeks, students examine their data and generate a hypothesis about the best ways for them to exercise. They design their individual routines, try them out, and analyze the results in terms of the perceived effectiveness of their new exercise routine.

Another option for designing projects around experimental inquiry is to have students analyze famous experiments in the past. For example, students might be asked to examine the Manhattan Project during World War II that resulted in the first atomic bombs. Students would be asked to describe:

- the observations that were made;
- the hypotheses that were generated;
- how the hypotheses were tested; and
- how theories were changed.

Perhaps the driving force in the experimental inquiry process is identifying previously unnoticed causal relationships. One of the most powerful parts of the process is that those hypothesized relationships are actually tested. The results of such testing not only foster insights about those relationships, but they also help students better understand characteristics of causal factors.

Investigation

An investigation is the process of identifying and then resolving differences of opinion or contradictory information about concepts, historical events, or possible future events. As this definition implies, there are three types of investigation tasks: definitional investigation, historical investigation, and projective investigation. These are defined more specifically in Table 7.1.

All three types of investigation can be likened to investigative reporting. To introduce the process, the teacher might relate how the investigation process discloses some common misconceptions about the development of the light bulb. The teacher explains that while most people believe that Thomas Edison

Table 7.1. *Three types of investigation*

Type of Investigation	Description
Definitional Investigation	Designing and defending a precise definition for a concept for which there are differing opinions and no generally agreed upon definition
Historical Investigation	Articulating and defending an explanation for a past event for which there are differing opinions as to what occurred and no generally agreed upon account of the event
Projective Investigation	Articulating and defending a prediction for a possible future event for which there are differing opinions as to what might occur and no generally agreed upon account

invented the "electric light," this is not accurate. The teacher explains that if you conducted a historical investigation, you would find that it is accurate to say that Edison produced the first commercially useful incandescent light bulb, but he was neither the first nor the only person who tried to develop an incandescent light bulb. Some historians assert that as many as 20 inventors had created versions prior to Edison's. Edison's version was able to outshine the others because of three factors: an effective incandescent filament, a better vacuum, and a system that made power distribution from a centralized source economically viable.

Using this example, the teacher would point out some of the defining features of an investigation, such as:

▶ It focuses on identifying the facts about a specific topic.
▶ It involves researching what people agree on and disagree on regarding a topic.
▶ It involves taking and defending a position.

The teacher would then provide students with a detailed set of steps for investigation:

1. Identify and describe:
   a. the concept you will define (definitional investigation);
   b. the past event you will explain (historical investigation); or
   c. the hypothetical event you will explain (projective investigation).
2. Describe what is generally known about or agreed upon about your concept, past event, or hypothetical event.
3. Describe what people disagree about or are confused about regarding your concept, past event, or hypothetical event.
4. Describe your position about the disagreements or confusions, and provide support for that position.

The teacher would then demonstrate the process using a concrete example. To illustrate, the teacher might relate a time when he became curious about the concept of old-growth forests. The teacher had moved to Oregon and kept hearing the term "old-growth forest" but really wasn't sure what it meant. He finally became curious enough that he started investigating the term. He found that it became popular in the 1970s when loggers in Oregon used it to describe forests that had reached substantial longevity without any substantial change to their ecosystems. Although this seemed intuitive and logical, when he dug further, he found there were a lot of issues about old-growth forests on which people disagreed, such as their common features. He continued researching enough about old-growth forests to come up with an answer to the common features question that satisfied him.

Once students have a working knowledge of the investigative process, the teacher can guide them in designing their own projects, like the following:

A geography teacher reminds students that they have been studying how human actions can impact the environment. The teacher tells students about a 1972 project off the coast of Florida during which 2 million old tires were dropped into the ocean about a mile off shore in an effort to create an artificial reef. Although the project was conceived with good intentions, it did not turn out well. In fact, the artificial reef turned out to be a huge environmental problem. Students are asked to investigate what happened and how the problem was addressed. They are asked to pay particular attention to the topics about which people don't agree, and to take a position about the issue and defend it.

Another option for designing projects is to have students study famous investigations such as the one conducted by Bob Woodward and Carl Bernstein around the Watergate scandal in the early 1970s. Students would be asked to:

▶ Describe the general findings articulated by Woodward and Bernstein.

▶ Describe how they collected their information.

▶ Describe controversies associated with Woodward and Bernstein's conclusions.

▶ State a position regarding one or more of the controversies and defend that position.

The investigation process directly fosters rigor by its emphasis on identifying and solving areas of disagreement or confusion. Students must discern characteristics about which they have not been previously aware and articulate support for those characteristics.

Invention

An invention involves the creation of a new process or product that meets a specific identified need. In a sense, it might be likened to problem-solving in that it addresses a specific need. However, problem-solving is limited in duration. Once the initial obstacle or limiting condition has been overcome, the problem-solving process ends. Invention commonly starts by trying to overcome a problem, but it continues over time as the new process or product gets refined.

The teacher might introduce the process of invention by providing an interesting example such as the invention of Post-it notes. In 1968, a scientist named Dr. Spencer Silver at the 3M company in the United States was trying to create a super-strong adhesive but one that took a little pressure before it adhered to a surface. His adhesive didn't receive much attention until 1974 when a friend named Art Fry came up with the idea of using the adhesive to replace his bookmark in his hymn book. Fry was so taken with the outcome that he started developing the idea. In 1977, 3M launched the "Press 'n Peel" bookmark. The color of the new bookmark was yellow simply because the development team only had yellow scrap paper with which to experiment. In 1979, the "Press 'n Peel" bookmark was sold as "Post-its" and their use has grown since then.

The teacher would use this example to discuss some of the defining characteristics of the invention process, such as:

▶ It comes from an observed need.

▶ Sometimes its development is serendipitous.

▶ It requires a number of iterations.

The teacher would then provide students with a detailed set of steps for an invention, such as the following:

1. Identify a situation you want to improve or a need you feel is unmet.

2. Describe the specific product or process you believe will improve the situation or satisfy the need.

3. Identify standards for your invention in terms of what it will do and how it will be used.

4. Make an initial sketch, model, or flowchart depicting your invention.

5. Begin developing your invention but continually look for ways to improve it as you go along. This might involve changing or adding to the standards you created in step #3.

6. When you've reached the point where your invention can be used, try it out with a small group or in a limited situation.

7. Reconsider your invention in light of your initial trials and make any modifications that seem necessary.

The teacher would then exemplify the steps of the process using a concrete example. For example, the teacher might tell a story about a person she knows who got frustrated when he cooked bacon and couldn't drain the grease without it getting all over the sink or the kitchen floor. The strainer he used drained the grease, but when he put the strainer in the sink, the grease clogged the pipes leading from the sink. He reasoned that if he could attach the strainer to a plate that had a lip on it, he could catch the grease and pour it into a plastic bag, which would go in the garbage. His criterion for success was simple: drain the bacon grease without spilling any. He drew a rough sketch of his idea, and then tried making the first version of his invention. He learned that fastening the strainer to a plate is the hardest obstacle to overcome. He eventually found a strainer and a plate with a lip that were made with the same type of plastic so that he could glue the strainer to the plate. The first version worked pretty well, but he ended up making a second version that improved on the previous version, one that was lighter and captured more grease.

Once students are aware of the invention process, the teacher would guide them in the design of tasks, such as the following:

> The teacher tells students to examine the process the school uses to distribute lunch and invent an alternative process that would make it more efficient. The students are told that they might not be able to actually use the process they have invented, but the class can discuss how feasible each proposed invention might be and present them to food services.

An alternative to creating projects around the invention process is to have students analyze historical inventions to ascertain how they followed the process. For example, students might be asked to examine the process Edison followed to come up with a filament that would last in his light bulb. Students would be asked to discuss:

- Early versions of the filament.
- Changes that were made in the various versions of the filament.
- The standards Edison set for the new invention.

The invention process fosters rigor by requiring students to set their own standards for what will make their invention acceptable. This means they have to think about their topic in new and different ways.

Systems Analysis

Systems analysis is the process of describing and analyzing the parts of a system with particular emphasis on the relationships among the parts. This process is commonly used when something breaks down in a system. For example, if your sprinkler system stops working in your backyard, you have to know how the system works before you can do anything to fix it. This is why we generally have to rely on experts to make such repairs.

The teacher might introduce this process by presenting students with some intriguing examples of systems, such as a prairie dog colony. If you walk by a prairie dog colony, it looks like a bunch of individualized mounds with prairie dogs standing alongside many of them. In fact, each mound represents a small group made up of an adult male, a few adult females, and their young that are less than two years old. These family units are called coteries. A prairie dog town or colony can be made up of thousands of coteries and millions of prairie dogs. When prairie dog colonies get relatively big, some of the prairie dogs take on different roles such as watching out for predators, conserving the food that is available, and acting as decoys. Colonies also have a definable social structure.

The teacher would use this example to discuss the defining features of systems analysis, including:

- defining the boundaries of the system;
- identifying the elements of the system; and
- identifying the causal relationships between elements.

The teacher would eventually provide students with a set of steps for systems analysis:

1. Identify a system to analyze and determine its boundaries (i.e., where it ends).
2. Identify the parts within the system and label each part.
3. For each part, describe its relationship with the other parts, paying particular attention to parts it directly affects and the parts it indirectly affects (i.e., through other parts) as well as parts that directly and indirectly affect it.
4. For each part, describe how changes in it affect the system as a whole.

The teacher would illustrate this process by using a concrete example. For example, the teacher might explain that after studying about systems, she realized that many aspects of her daily life involve a system, such as the coffee shop she goes to. The coffee shop system begins at the end of the line where you place your order. As you move up in line, you need to get your order ready so that you can give it to the people behind the counter. Your order can trigger three possible actions on the part of the people behind the counter. A coffee order is filled by one person, an order involving a bagel involves another person, and an order that involves a heated bagel with something on it involves still another person. When you get your order and pay for it, then you progress to the phase of the system where you get your utensils, cream, sugar, and condiments. Next, you progress to the eating phase. The final phase involves disposing of your garbage. Once students have a general understanding of the systems analysis process, the teacher guides them in the design of tasks like the following:

> The teacher reminds students that they have been studying open systems which, by definition, exchange matter and energy with their surroundings. She tells them to pick one of the open systems they have been studying and describe the boundaries, the component parts, and how those parts interact.

Another option for using systems analysis for projects involves having students analyze historical attempts to understand a system. For example, the teacher might have students examine the development of our current conception of the solar system. Students would be asked to report on:

- How notions of the parts of the solar system have changed.
- How notions of the boundaries of the solar system have changed.
- How notions of the relationships between the planets and the Sun have changed.

The systems analysis process enhances rigor because it requires students to make new distinctions. This occurs when students label each part of the system. It also requires them to articulate relationships. This occurs as students describe how each part of the system affects and is affected by other parts.

Students Creating Their Own Projects

As soon as possible, students should generate their own projects in an environment that affords them as many options as possible. Once students have been introduced to the various knowledge application processes described previously, they can select the process they would like to use for their projects. The planning questions in Table 7.2 can be used to this end.

To create projects, students could ask these questions in the context of a specific subject area to generate ideas for projects. For example, at the beginning of the second semester, a literature teacher might have students ask these questions as tools for creating their own projects. One student might find she would like to study a decision that was made to ban a specific book in the district (decision-making). Another student might find that he wants to investigate the final days of Ernest Hemingway's life leading up to his suicide (historical investigation), and so on. Students would use the steps described in this chapter to structure their projects.

Table 7.2. *Planning questions for projects*

Problem-Solving:

- Is there a problem that I would like to solve and for which I would defend my solution?
- Is there a problem that has been solved that I would like to analyze?

Decision-Making:

- Is there a decision I would like to make and defend?
- Is there a decision that has been made that I would like to analyze?

Investigation:

- Is there an unresolved issue about the defining characteristics of something (definitional), or why or how something happened (historical), or what might occur under specific circumstances (projective) I would like to study?
- Is there an investigation that has already been conducted about the defining characteristics of something (definitional), or why or how something happened (historical), or what might occur under specific conditions (projective) I would like to analyze?

Experimental Inquiry:

- Is there a prediction that I would like to make and test?
- Is there an experiment that has already been conducted that I would like to analyze?

Invention:

- Is there a situation I would like to improve on by creating something new?
- Is there an invention I would like to analyze?

Systems Analysis:

- Is there a system I would like to analyze?
- Is there an analysis of a system I would like to study?

Epilogue

In this book, I have attempted to describe a comprehensive approach to enhancing rigor in the classroom. I have defined rigor in specific ways. As articulated in the introductory chapter, rigor involves discerning new relationships between topics and new distinctions within topics. It also involves discerning new distinctions about oneself as a learner.

I have tried to provide enough guidance and concrete examples so that individual teachers can design activities that will enhance the rigor with which students engage with content. My ultimate goal in writing this book is that entire schools or, better yet, school systems create comprehensive K–12 curriculums that ensure students graduate with the necessary skills for success in the work force, in the academic world, and most importantly, for success at the enduring and transcendental aspects of life as they individually define them.

References

Blackburn, B. R. (2008). *Rigor is not a four-letter word*. New York, NY: Eye On Education.

Good, T. L., & Brophy, J. E. (2003). *Learning in classroom* (9th ed.) Boston, MA: Allyn & Bacon.

Hechinger Institute. (2009). *Understanding and reporting on academic rigor*. Retrieved from Teachers College, Columbia University website: http://hechinger.tc.columbia .edu/primers/Hechinger_Institute_Rigor_Primer.pdf

Kintsch, W. (1974). *The representation of meaning in memory*. Hillsdale, NJ: Lawrence Erlbaum Associates.

Kintsch, W. (1979). On modeling comprehension. *Educational Psychologist, 14*(1), 3–14.

Kintsch, W., & van Dijk, T. A. (1978). Toward a model of text comprehension and production. *Psychological Review, 85*(5), 363–394.

Marzano, R. J. (1992). *A different kind of classroom: Teaching with dimensions of learning*. Alexandria, VA: ASCD.

Marzano, R. J. (2018). *The new art and science of teaching*. Bloomington, IN: Solution Tree Press.

Marzano, R. J., Brandt, R. S., Hughes, C. S., Jones, B. F., Presseisen, B. Z., Rankin, S. C., & Suhor, C. (1988). *Dimensions of thinking: A framework for curriculum and instruction*. Alexandria, VA: ASCD.

Marzano, R. J., Norford, J. S., & Ruyle, M. (2019). *The new art and science of classroom assessment*. Bloomington, IN: Solution Tree Press.

Marzano, R. J., & Pickering, D. J. (1997). *Dimensions of learning: Teacher's manual* (2nd ed.). Alexandria, VA: ASCD.

Marzano, R. J., & Simms, J. A. (2014). *Questioning sequences in the classroom*. Bloomington, IN: Marzano Research Laboratory.

McNulty, R. J., & Quaglia, R. J. (2007). Rigor, relevance, and relationships. *School Administrator, 64*(8), 18–23.

McREL International. (2014a). Content knowledge: Online edition. Retrieved from www2.mcrel.org/compendium/browse.asp

McREL International. (2014b). Content knowledge: Online edition. The process of this work. Retrieved from http://www2.mcrel.org/compendium/docs/process.asp

National Research Council. (2004). Box 3.1. Buggy algorithms. In M. S. Donovan & J. W. Pellegrino (Eds.), *Learning and instruction: A SERP research agenda*. Retrieved from www.nap.edu/read/10858/chapter/5

Redfield, D. L., & Rousseau, E. W. (1981). A meta-analysis of experimental research on teacher questioning behavior. *Review of Educational Research, 51*(1), 237–245.

Wagner, T. (2008a). *The global achievement gap: Why even our best schools don't teach the new survival skills our children need—and what we can do about it.* New York, NY: Basic Books.

Wagner, T. (2008b). Rigor redefined. *Educational Leadership, 66*(2), 20–24.

We All Can Read. (n.d.). How to sound out words. Retrieved February 1, 2019, from https://weallcanread.com/how-to-sound-out-words/

Wilen, W. W., & Clegg, A. A. (1986). Effective questions and questioning: A research review. *Theory and Research in Social Education, 14*(2), 153–161.

Williamson, R., & Johnston, J. H. (1999). Challenging orthodoxy: An emerging agenda for middle level reform. *Middle School Journal, 30*(4), 10–17.

Winne, P. H. (1979). Experiments relating teachers' use of higher cognitive questions to student achievement. *Review of Educational Research, 49*(1), 13–50.